Savor
the Shore

Special Thanks

The Press of Atlantic City wishes to acknowledge the many people who helped make this publication possible. Tom Briglia, our photographer, deserves a world of thanks for taking amazing photos and patiently traveling all over Southern New Jersey. A big thank you goes to Jeanne Donohue for rewriting all the reviews used in the book. Thank you to Linda Gallagher for her editing skills. Also, an enormous thank you goes to Steve Warren, Steve Cronin and Scott Cronick from our Editorial Department for their support and recommendations. Michelle Boggs deserves to be recognized for organizing all the book orders and her administrative support. Special thanks to project coordinator Jamie Hoagland. Lastly, this book could not have been done with out the support from all the restaurants. Thank you to the chefs, owners, managers, and staff who always took the time to answer the countless phone calls and emails to clarify the tiniest of details. The Press of Atlantic City hopes everyone has as much fun making these wonderful recipes as we did collecting them.

Published by Pediment Publishing, a division of The Pediment Group, Inc.   www.pediment.com Printed in Canada.

Foreword

There are lots of reasons to love the southern New Jersey shore—great beaches, beautiful vistas, lots of fun things to do.

But many who vacation here come for another reason entirely—to eat some really great meals. It's no surprise that the shore area is home to quality seafood restaurants or that Atlantic City's casinos host restaurants by some of the top names in the food business. But even our "family" restaurants are known to serve up meals that match in inventiveness and quality whatever you might order in Philadelphia or New York.

From Cape May to Atlantic City to Long Beach Island, there's top-notch dining with enough choices to please any discriminating palate.

For this book, we asked some of our area's most highly regarded restaurants and chefs to share some of their most popular recipes.

From the Atlantic Monkfish Tagine served at Seablue in the Borgata to the Butternut Squash Soup that can be ordered at Sea Salt in Stone Harbor, the recipes are indicative of the many dining choices our area offers.

Think of this book as the ultimate southern New Jersey menu sampler. There's enough here to give those who cook many happy hours in the kitchen and at the table. And for those who prefer to make reservations, think of browsing through these pages as the first step in ordering another memorable meal at the shore.

Steve Cronin
Features Editor
The Press of Atlantic City

Table of Contents

Andrea Trattoria Italiana

With a small, homey dining room, crisp white tablecloths and red glass candleholders, Andrea Trattoria Italiana has the feel of taverns in Italy. Chef Andrea Covina cooks from his soul.

Focaccia and herb-and-oil dipping sauce are offered while diners peruse the menu. Seafood is a star, with some dishes finished tableside. Speck appetizer is reminiscent of smoked prosciutto, sliced paper-thin and piled on a bed of citrus-coated baby arugula with slices of tomato and fresh mozzarella.

An appetizer of ragu di funghi con polenta is a simple preparation of grilled polenta with wild mushrooms and a light tomato sauce with basil.

Chilean sea bass makes a memorable entrée, served with a crispy potato crust and a sauce of fresh tomato, capers, basil, slices of garlic and extra virgin olive oil.

Enjoy a wonderful cappuccino while choosing from a long list of homemade desserts—including limoncello soufflé, creamy and rich like gelati with a lemony zing.

Come on in!

Address:
1883 Harding Highway
Newfield

Phone:
856-697-8400

Gamberi Al Prosciutto con Avocado

Shrimp Wrapped in Prosciutto Served with an Avocado Salad

Ingredients / Serves 2

6 slices parma prosciutto
6 jumbo shrimp (cleaned and deveined)
1 avocado sliced
½ lemon sliced
6 cherry tomatoes cut in half
¼ red onion sliced
¼ cup extra virgin olive oil
salt and pepper to taste

SALAD: In a mixing bowl, toss avocado, cherry tomatoes, red onions, lemon juice and salt and pepper. Arrange cherry tomatoes with avocado in center.

SHRIMP: Wrap shrimp in prosciutto. Heat oil in pan at medium heat until hot. Sear shrimp on one side for about two minutes until prosciutto is crispy. Do the same on the other side. Plate the shrimp around tomatoes and avocado.

Athenian Garden

Whet your appetite by watching the pita bread sizzle and flames lick delicious looking kabobs on the grill. Athenian Garden has a buzzing open kitchen to watch and a pleasant, family-run atmosphere to enjoy.

The dining room is light and bright with hardwood floors, sturdy pine tables and framed photos of Greece on yellow walls.

Tasty toasted pita dipped into tzatziki sauce, a marriage of fresh cucumber and sour cream, makes a great starter.

An appetizer of calamari, fried in a light coating and served with a touch of lemon on top, is perfect in its simplicity. Spanakotiropita, two large triangles of warm phyllo dough surrounding spinach and feta cheese, is Greek food at its finest.

Mousaka, a thick slice of baked eggplant topped with layers of spicy ground beef in tomato sauce and slices of potato, then finished with creamy béchamel sauce and melted feta cheese, is a classic. Topping it off with a homemade baklava dessert makes for a complete, authentic Greek experience.

Come on in!

Address:
619 Route 9
Galloway Township

Phone:
609-748-1818

Tsipoura Plaki

Oven Baked Royal Daurade

Ingredients / Serves 4

1 large onion, cut in half and thinly sliced

4-5 cloves of garlic thinly sliced

5-7 tablespoons extra virgin olive oil

2/3 cup of Kalamata olives (pitted)

1 Royal Daurade 3.5-4 pound, cleaned (*fish, also called bream or porgy)

coarse sea salt and fresh ground pepper

1 large pinch mixed dried herbs – Greek oregano, thyme, and marjoram

1 pound fresh tomatoes, peeled and seeded, cut into wedges

1 green frying pepper and 1 red bell pepper seeded, deribbed and cut into long narrow strips

¾ cup dry white wine

Preheat oven to 400 degrees.

Pour 2 tablespoons of extra virgin olive oil in a medium sized frying pan at high temperature. Sauté the tomatoes for 2 minutes then add ¼ cup of white wine. Then add the thinly sliced garlic and reduce for another 1 to 2 minutes. Set aside.

Pour 1 tablespoon of extra virgin olive oil in the bottom of a large gratin dish, coating the bottom. Place thinly sliced onions in the gratin dish. Rub the entire fish inside and out with extra virgin olive oil. Season the fish inside and out to taste with sea salt, ground pepper and mixed dried herbs. Place fish on top of the onions and scatter the Kalamata olives and sliced peppers on top of the fish. Scatter the sautéed tomatoes and garlic over the fish. Pour remaining wine in the bottom of the dish and dribble any remaining olive oil on top of the fish.

Place in the oven and bake for 35-40 minutes, basting a couple of times after the first 20 minutes. Test for doneness with a sharp skewer. Serve directly from gratin dish moving vegetables aside. Cut into bone along the lateral line. Slit the skin next to the fins and all the length of the back and from the abdomen to the tail. Then cut across and lift up serving portions with a spatula. Accompany each serving with vegetables and juices.

COMPLEMENTING DRINK: Boutari Moschofilero

COOKING TIP: When cooking with garlic, cut in half vertically and remove the white vein-like piece in the middle. Doing this helps prevent heartburn.

Basilico's Ristorante & Pizzeria

This is Italian cuisine at its classic, simple best, from pizza and stromboli to stuffed shells. Make sure to try the real stars, like Vitello Basilica, veal sautéed and served with lumb crabmeat and artichoke hearts in a basil cream sauce.

Chef Scott Oliver named Pescatore Passomonti for his mother, whose maiden name was Passomonti. It is a seafood pasta medley of little neck clams, mussels, shrimp and a strip of salmon fillet sautéed in oil and garlic and served in a blush sauce over linguine.

The shellfish in its shells is fresh and beautifully seasoned. Tender and tasty, the salmon is complemented nicely by the blush sauce.

The little details make the meal wonderful, like the dipping sauce for the sesame bread, with its hint of oil, vinegar, and spices. Homemade sweet Vidalia onion house dressing is delicious enough to drink on its own.

Come on in!

Address:
27 43rd Street
Sea Isle City

Phone:
609-263-1010

Basilico's Pescatore Passomonti

Ingredients / Serves 4

4 tablespoons extra virgin olive oil
18 clams scrubbed
1 tablespoon garlic, chopped
2 tablespoons chopped scallions
1 cup fresh diced tomatoes
½ cup white wine
2 cups fish stock or clam juice
28 mussels
8 ounces scallops
12 jumbo shrimp, cleaned, peeled, and deveined
2 cups tomato sauce
1 pound linguine pasta
2 ounce butter, cubed
¼ cup chopped fresh herbs — parsley, basil, and thyme

Heat oil in hot pan. Add clams, garlic, and scallions, sauté approximately three minutes. Add tomatoes, white wine, and fish stock. Cook until clams open.

Add sea scallops, mussels, shrimp, and tomato sauce. Cook for approximately three minutes.

Bring six quarts of salted water to a boil. Cook linguine pasta seven to nine minutes until al dente. Drain well. Place in four hot bowls. Arrange seafood around bowls. Add butter and herbs to sauce. Stir until butter is incorporated. Spoon over pasta and garnish with fresh basil or thyme.

WINE PAIRING: Santa Margherita Pinot Grigio

COOKING TIP: Zap garlic cloves in the microwave for fifteen seconds and the skins will slip right off.

Beach Creek Oyster Bar & Grille

The deck is the place to be at Beach Creek Oyster Bar and Grille. Pretend you're sitting on a yacht. At sunset, watch the neighboring paddle-wheeled riverboat take off on a cruise. The inside dining room glows with a romantic air. Neat wooden booths front many windows for a view of the sunset.

Arrive hungry: The dishes are colorful and well-seasoned. The good-sized portions are a pleasure to devour.

True to the name, choose oysters on the half shell or all gussied up. Prussian Pearls are six Cape May Salts—prized Delaware Bay oysters—splashed with vodka and topped with sour cream, diced red onion and black caviar.

Jersey tomato is featured in a terrific slice of baked tomato, walnuts, fresh basil and provolone cheese on a flaky pie crust. A new addition to the menu is tomato-basil grouper. Chef Jim Koch pairs the sweet, meaty fish with a local produce treasure, served over cheese risotto and garlic sautéed spinach.

Come on in!

Address:
500 W. Hand Avenue
Wildwood

Phone:
609-522-1062

Beach Creek's Tomato Basil Grouper
Grouper Fillets with Balsamic Roasted Jersey Tomatoes and Basil

Ingredients / Serves 4

2 large fresh Jersey tomatoes
½ red onion
6 leaves of fresh basil
1 lemon
½ ounce balsamic vinegar
1 ounce extra virgin olive oil
Salt & ground black pepper to taste
4-8 ounce pieces of grouper

TOMATO-BASIL TOPPING: Cut tomatoes in large dice.

Thinly slice the red onion into ½ moon slices.

Stack the basil leaves and roll them into a cigar shape, then slice into thin strips.

Cut the lemon in thin wheel slices (remove any seeds).

Place prepared ingredients in a bowl and toss with the vinegar & olive oil.

Season with salt & fresh ground pepper to taste.

The tomato mix can be used right away, but is better if you let it marinate for at least an hour, and best if let to sit refrigerated over night.

GROUPER: Lightly season the fillets with salt & fresh ground pepper before placing them in a lightly oiled baking dish. Top the fillets with the tomato basil topping and bake in a pre-heated oven at 400 degrees until fish is cooked through and begins to flake.

Serve over cheese risotto and garlic sautéed spinach, or with white rice or pasta.

This recipe would also work well with other white fish including halibut, cod, flounder, and striper.

WINE PAIRING: Portalupi Pinot Noir

COOKING TIP: To extend the life of fresh herbs, wrap roots in a damp paper towel and place in the refrigerator.

Blue

In this modern-retro chic dining room with glowing hardwood floors, cozy booths and colorful local and international surfing artwork on the walls, sit back and prepare to enjoy globally influenced, eclectic American cuisine—a fusion of Latino, Mediterranean, Asian, and French.

Blue is inspired by warm climates, its simple name referring to the color, beauty and inspiration of sea and sky. Head Chef Steven Cameron develops a menu that takes advantage of the seasons with an emphasis on using local ingredients.

Owners Todd Rodgers and Bruno Pouget

insist seafood be front and center. Warm mussel salad and Maine lobster salad are popular starters. Try the grilled Barnegat Light tuna or scallops for a sample of the day's catch.

Save room for dessert: If you're lucky, warm chocolate cake with mango and carrot cake with pineapple might be among the choices.

Come on in!

Address:
1016 Long Beach Boulevard
Surf City

Phone:
609-494-7556

Web:
www.bluelbi.com

Wild East Coast Black Bass

Pan-roasted Wild East Coast Black Bass with Summer Potato Salad and Sauce Vierge

SUMMER POTATO SALAD

1 pound purple peruvian fingerling potatoes, washed

½ pound haricot vert, trimmed

1 shallot, peeled

5 garlic cloves, peeled

1 sprig thyme

½ red onion, shaved very thin on mandoline

½ tablespoon tarragon, chiffonade

½ tablespoon thyme, minced

¼ cup crème fraîche

⅛ cup mayonnaise

1 tablespoon lemon juice, fresh

1 tablespoon chives, chiffonade

1 tablespoon parsley, chiffonade

SAUCE VIERGE

2 red tomatoes, large, ripe, peeled, seeded

2 garlic cloves, peeled, grated on microplane

½ cup extra virgin olive oil

1 tablespoon lemon juice, fresh

1 tablespoon red wine vinegar, fresh

20 basil leaves, chiffonade

BLACK BASS

1 black bass, descaled, gutted, about 3 pounds

1 tablespoon cooking oil

SUMMER POTATO SALAD: In a large pot, bring heavily salted water to a boil and blanch haricot vert until bright green and slightly tender. Remove to an ice bath to preserve color and stop cooking. Drain and cut into 1½-inch pieces. Keep chilled.

In a medium pot, place whole potatoes, shallot, garlic and thyme in cold, salted water and place over medium heat. Bring water to a simmer and cook until the potatoes are almost tender. Let potatoes cool in water to absorb aromatics. Drain and chill. Throw away the aromatics. Cut fingerlings into 1/8-inch coins.

Combine all ingredients with the potato and haricot vert just before service. Season with salt and white pepper.

SAUCE VIERGE: Gently warm extra virgin olive oil with microplaned garlic. Add tomatoes and warm extremely gently. Imagine that you are releasing the flavor of the tomatoes slowly as opposed to cooking them. Cool and fold in lemon juice and vinegar. Season with salt and white pepper. Add basil. Should have the consistency of a thick vinaigrette.

BLACK BASS: Fillet the black bass and remove the pinbones. One fillet on a 3 pound fish should yield two 6-ounce portions.

Heat oil in a heavy sauté pan or iron skillet until very hot but not smoking. Season the fish on both sides and lay the fish skin-side down in the oil. Gently press the fish with your fingers until the skin relaxes and lays flat, so as to evenly crisp. If the oil is not hot enough the fish will stick! If it is too hot the skin will burn. Leave on heat until the skin is well browned and place skillet in a 275 degree oven to gently cook to medium. Remove and pat remaining oil off with a paper towel.

Place ½ cup of potato salad on four plates. Place warm bass on top and drizzle sauce vierge about the plate. Garnish with micro basil.

DRINK PAIRING: For the black bass dish, I would recommend something fun and refreshing, like a Basque Txakolina. It is an acidic, semi-sparkling Spanish white from Pais Basco that will highlight the lemony, herbal and fresh summer ingredients well.

COOKING TIP: Slow food is important, from cultivating and processing fresh ingredients to the actual cooking and preparation. Poaching, braising or roasting food at, say, 225 degrees instead of 350 degrees means that the interior of the food will eventually reach the desired temperature without the exterior overcooking. A hot oven will cause the flesh of a delicate and delicious black bass to seize up. Take time when you cook and experience what you are actually doing with friends and family.

Braca Café

Braca Café still wins over diners more than 100 years after it opened its doors. The ingredients for its success: wonderful food; clean, comfortable atmosphere and friendly, efficient table service.

Established in the early 1900s by the grandfather of the current owner, Braca specializes in great pasta and fresh seafood, although there are plenty of other things on the menu. Start by nibbling on fresh bread dipped in olive oil with roasted red peppers.

Some of many standout dishes: Lemon garlic chicken, a roasted breast served over mashed potatoes with lemon jus, spinach and grape tomatoes; and black peppercorn fettucine, pasta in a dill cream sauce with grape tomatoes and salmon morsels.

Come on in!

Address:
Kennedy Boulevard & the beach
Sea Isle City

Phone:
609-263-4271

Web:
www.bracacafe.com

Scallops Penne'

Ingredients / Serves 2

SCALLOPS

4 scallops (large size, 10 per pound)
2 ounces cajun spices
2 ounces clarified butter

SAUCE

2 tablespoons extra virgin olive oil
2 cloves garlic (sliced thin)
6 ounces San Marzano tomatoes (hand crushed)
3 ounces heavy cream
3 ounces reggiano parmigiano, grated
1 cup fresh spinach
salt and pepper to taste

Coat scallops lightly with cajun spices, then roll in clarified butter. Sear on a smoking hot cast-iron skillet, two minutes each side. Set aside.

In a hot sauté pan, sauté garlic in olive oil until light golden color. Add heavy cream and tomatoes. Reduce four minutes. Toss in spinach, cheese, salt and pepper and reduce three minutes. Toss with favorite al dente pasta. Top with scallops and garnish with fresh basil leaves.

WINE RECOMMENDATION: Estancia Chardonnay

COOKING TIP: Dry your scallops before cooking.

Buddakan

Enter Buddakan through an enchanted Asian garden surrounded by multi-colored archways, 25-foot-tall trees that appear to grow through the ceiling, rocks, and foot bridges.

In the awe-inspiring dining room, a giant golden Buddha looms at the end of a lighted onyx communal table, keeping watch over all.

In the dining room, it's easy to imagine you are eating in the courtyard of an ancient Chinese building, under a starry twilight sky. Or enjoy privacy in one of the curtained opium-den-style nooks. Upstairs, private rooms have walls that look like Japanese sand gardens.

Modern Asian fare matches the stunning décor. Signature dishes include tuna spring roll; edamame ravioli with truffled Sautérnes-shallot broth; crispy calamari salad featuring bitter greens and miso dressing; pan-seared sea bass on a bed of haricot verts, maitake mushrooms and a truffle jus, and chargrilled aged beef with Szechuan fries and a watercress salad.

Come on in!

Address:
The Pier at Caesars
Atlantic City

Phone:
609-674-0100

Web:
www.buddakanac.com

Hot & Sour Sea Scallops

5 Dry Sea Scallops
 ounce of corn
½ ounce of Chinese sausage small dice (If not
  available use hard salami)
 ounce Tofu (small dice)
 ounce black trumpet mushroom
 tablespoon cilantro (sliced)
 tablespoon scallion (sliced)
2 tablespoons soybean oil
 tablespoon extra virgin olive oil
 teaspoon fresh lime juice

HOT AND SOUR BROTH

3 cups of chicken broth
¼ cup soy sauce
¼ rice wine vinegar
2 teaspoons sambal (or a hot chili paste)
½ cup cornstarch (see recipe)

HOT AND SOUR BROTH: Place chicken broth in the pot and bring to a boil. (Have the rest of the products measured out and ready to add to the broth.) When the broth has come to a boil add the rest of the ingredients except the cornstarch and bring the liquid to a simmer. Add some water to the cornstarch in a separate bowl just to loosen the lumps and make smooth. Add the cornstarch mixture to the liquid, whisking until slightly thick. Cool down.

COOKING SCALLOPS: First select firm scallops and remove the side muscle that is attached. Dry. Season both sides of the scallops with salt. Warm the skillet for about one minute and add the oil to the pan. Wait for the oil to get a little hot, and add the scallops to the pan. Let the scallops caramelize with a little bit of color before turning over in the hot skillet. (Make sure the skillet is tilted away from you when turning over the scallops to prevent oil splatter). Turn off heat from under the skillet and let the residual heat cook the scallops for about 30 seconds longer so it gets a perfect medium rare to medium. Take scallops out of the skillet and place on a plate with a paper towel to absorb moisture.

In a sauce pan add the Hot and Sour Broth and place the corn, tofu, Chinese sausage, black mushroom, scallion and cilantro. Bring to a simmer. In a bowl add broth and place the scallops on top. Drizzle a little bit of the olive oil and lime juice on the scallops.

DRINK PAIRING: "Hugel" Gewurztraminer.

Café 2825

Simple, really. That's what makes great Italian food at Café 2825. Start with bright green, good, fruity olive oil poured on a plate for dipping the warm, crispy Italian loaf. Traditional dishes such as tripe in marinara sauce with baby green peas and roasted shallot are comfortable alongside more modern ones like grilled octopus over grilled slices of yellow squash. Nicely crisp around the tentacles after a quick bath in olive oil and served with a balsamic sauce and a slice of lemon.

Pork Chop Milanaise is a bone-in center-cut pork chop pounded thin and dredged through herb-and-cheese-seasoned bread crumbs, then pan fried. Finish with a crisp cannoli stuffed with ricotta cheese mixture with lots of chocolate chips and dusted with powdered sugar. Again, simple and good.

The café has the feel of a family trattoria with framed pictures of relatives on the walls. The owner is likely to stop by your table while you're there.

Come on in!

Address:
2825 Atlantic Avenue
Atlantic City

Phone:
609-344-6913

Clams Oreganata
Baked Stuffed Italian Style Littleneck Clams

Ingredients / Serves 2

16 little neck clams
1 cup clam juice mix
½ bunch chopped parsley
½ teaspoon dry oregano
2 tablespoons grated romano
1 clove garlic, sliced thin
½ teaspoon salt
½ teaspoon black pepper
3 cups seasoned Italian breadcrumbs
¼ cup olive oil

Steam clams until open with 1 cup water. Save juice. Mix parsley through olive oil together in a bowl and then stuff each steamed clam with one tablespoon mix. Place on cookie pan and bake until breadcrumbs have browned at 450 degrees. Add clam juice to bottom of cookie pan. When serving, top with 1 teaspoon of pan juice on each clam.

WINE PAIRING: Italian white Michele Chiarlo.

COOKING TIP: Keep in mind when purchasing ground beef—the more lean the beef, the less flavorful and moist. For burgers, chuck is the most flavorful.

Carrabba's Italian Grill

At Carrabba's Italian Grill, find smiling faces, efficient service and delicious, interesting food. From the dining room, watch the flame and steam from the open kitchen as the chef turns out good, not fancy food.

Start with a hot quarter-loaf of sliced Tuscan and a plate of parsley, basil, hot pepper flakes and garlic swirled by the server with olive oil. Portions are huge, the soups fantastic—lentil and sausage is stellar—and salads crisp and fresh.

From the wood-burning grill comes Spiedino Di Mare—scallops and shrimp grilled in a light coating of Italian breadcrumbs and

served with a lemon butter sauce.

Among the memory-makers are the house-made desserts, including Dessert Rosa, a layered sponge cake with banana, strawberry and pineapple, vanilla pudding and topped with a chocolate covered cherry.

Come on in!

Address:
6725 Black Horse Pike
Egg Harbor Township

Phone:
609-407-2580

Web:
www.carrabbas.com

Salmon Cetriolini

Fresh Salmon Grilled and Topped with Diced Tomatoes and Seeded Cucumber in a Lemon Butter Dill Sauce

Ingredients / Serves 4

4 salmon fillets
2 ounces extra virgin olive oil
pinch salt
pinch pepper

CETRIOLINI SAUCE

½ cup Roma tomatoes (¼ inch dice)
½ cup cucumbers (peeled, seeded, and ¼ inch dice)
1 tablespoon fresh dill (chopped fine)
2 tablespoons extra virgin olive oil
1 tablespoon lemon juice
pinch salt
pinch pepper

SALMON: Season salmon fillets with salt and pepper. Then brush with extra virgin olive oil and grill or broil in oven to desired doneness. About 10-12 minutes.

CETRIOLINI SAUCE: In a mixing bowl combine all ingredients and mix. Season with the salt and pepper to taste. Then ladle over the top of the grilled salmon.

WINE PAIRING: Clos du Bois Russian River Chardonnay – This aromatic Chardonnay explodes with aromas of citrus, ripe pear and lime with jasmine and spice overtones. The vibrant acidity will enhance the fresh flavors of the Cetriolini sauce and the lush, well integrated oak and smooth creamy texture should compliment the smoky richness of the salmon very well.

COOKING TIP: When working with garlic it tends to linger on the hands. To remove the odor, wash hands with soap and water. Then rub hands on something made of stainless steel (bowl, sink basin, or utensil). This will alchemize the odor.

Chef Vola

Few of Atlantic City's quirky landmarks are as enduring and endearing as Chef Vola. The family-run restaurant is notoriously hard to find, with an unmarked, below-street-level entrance and an unlisted telephone number.

If you are lucky enough to find it and enter the low-ceilinged, unpretentious dining room, owner Louise Esposito and her staff treat you like family. Stucco and wood-beamed walls, old photographs, Italian background music and white linen table-cloths all add to a timeless quality.

Dinners are wonderfully good and sinfully large. Angel hair pasta with white clam sauce and veal with prosciutto and provolone are two dishes not to miss.

Save room for dessert. Louise Esposito must spend half her life baking, with delicious results. Two of the best—ricotta cake flavored with rum and butterscotch and a cream pie flavored with limoncello and the zest and juice from lemons.

Come on in!

Address:
111 South Albion Place
Atlantic City

Phone:
609-345-2022

Capellini with Shrimp

Capellini with Colossal Shrimp and Jumbo Lump Crabmeat in Marinara Sauce

Ingredients / Serves 4

½ pound jumbo lump crabmeat
1 pound colossal peeled and deveined shrimp
¼ cup fresh Italian parsley
3 sprigs fresh basil
1 pound capellini
½ brown onion diced

MARINARA SAUCE (1 QT.)

¼ cup extra virgin olive oil
7 cloves garlic, peeled and sliced thin
½ teaspoon crushed red pepper flakes
1 35-ounce can crushed Italian plum
    tomatoes, in liquid
½ teaspoon dried oregano, marjoram, basil,
    and rosemary
pinch salt
½ cup clam juice

MARINARA SAUCE: Heat extra virgin olive oil in a large skillet over medium heat. Add garlic and onions until golden brown. Sprinkle in dry herbs and red pepper flakes. Pour in crushed tomatoes. Add clam juice. Simmer for about an hour.

SEAFOOD: After marinara has simmered for an hour, add shrimp into the sauce with fresh parsley and basil sprigs. Simmer 15 minutes

PASTA: Bring 6 quarts of water to a boil in an 8-quart pot over high heat with a pinch of salt. Add capellini, stir frequently. Cook about 3 to 4 minutes until al dente. Drain thoroughly and return to pot. Add crabmeat. Pour marinara sauce and shrimp over capellini. Add fresh basil leaf for garnish.

FINISH: Place pasta in large oval serving dish, top with crabmeat and shrimp.

Daddy O Hotel & Restaurant

An eatery chic enough to be on Times Square instead of on the beach, Daddy O has a modern, edgy interior. Deep reds, browns and blacks are the colors of the plush booths and rich leather chairs. Striking light fixtures include spiky balls and silvery, confetti-shaped sculptures.

Highlights of the extremely continental cuisine are Jamaican BBQ-roasted chicken breast and filet mignon with roasted garlic potatoes. Mandarin pork tenderloin is a chef's specialty. And, of course, there are seafood choices such as pan-roasted red snapper with steamed mussels, olive oil mashed potatoes and white wine lemon butter.

Food preparation and presentation matches the modern setting. Portions are artfully stacked, lined up and drizzled. Traditional favorites are turned out in ways you've never seen, such as "buffalo wingless"—an appetizer of boneless tempura chicken, Vietnamese chili sauce and micro celery.

A slice of cappuccino chocolate cheesecake or an Irish coffee topped with whipped cream is a sweet end to an amazing meal.

Come on in!

Address:
4401 Long Beach Boulevard
Brant Beach

Phone:
609-494-1300

Mandarin Pork Tenderloin

3 pounds pork tenderloin, cleaned or pork loin sliced into 1-inch-thick slices

MARINADE

1 cup soy sauce

2 tablespoons brown sugar

4 each garlic cloves, rough chopped

1 tablespoon ginger, peeled, diced

1 cup balsamic vinegar

2 each jalapeno

2 sprigs rosemary

1 sprig thyme

1 cup water

STIR FRY VEGETABLES

2 each baby bok choy

1 each red pepper, cut into 1 inch long, thin strips

1 each yellow pepper, cut into 1 inch long, thin strips

1 bunch broccoli, cut into small florets

2 each carrots, cut into thin strips

1 each garlic, minced

DUMPLINGS

2 each Idaho potatoes

2 each egg yolks

½ cup all purpose flour

½ cup rice flour

salt & pepper to taste

SESAME SOY GLAZE

2 cups balsamic vinegar

3 cups soy sauce

½ cup sugar

4 tablespoons sesame oil

2 tablespoons corn starch

2 tablespoons water

MARINADE: Combine all ingredients in a large bowl and mix well. In another container, completely submerge pork, cover and refrigerate overnight or 1 day. Before cooking, remove pork from marinade, pat dry with a paper towel to remove excess moisture, and reserve marinade for next use.

STIR FRY VEGETABLES: Wash bok choy under cold running water to remove dirt; drain. Cut off bottom 'white' part, then chiffonade or cut into thin 'strips'. In a bowl or container add other vegetables except garlic. In a medium sauté pan, allow pan to heat on medium heat. Add a small amount of blended or vegetable oil, add stir fry vegetables and stir to ensure even cooking. Add minced garlic and sauté until garlic is golden brown, salt and pepper to taste.*** Note: Vegetables can be prepared 1 day ahead, but should be cooked prior to serving. Also, vegetables should be cooked quickly to ensure bright color and texture; overcooking will cause vegetables to become bland and mushy.

DUMPLINGS: In a large pot of boiling water, boil potatoes in their skins, until fork tender. Drain potatoes, peel skins and rice through a food mill or crush potatoes with fork; allow to cool. On a flat table top or counter, dust surface with small amount flour, form potatoes into mound, then create a well or hole in the center. Add egg yolks, salt and pepper, and add at small amounts of flour at a time, and knead flour and potatoes together. Add remaining flour as needed until firm, but not hard, consistency (almost like fresh pasta) and allow dough to rest and cool.

When cooled, roll dough into long segments(about thickness of a quarter, and about 12 inches in length. Cut into small sections about a 1 inch long. In a small pot of boiling, salted water drop dumplings and allow to cook until they float to top. Note: Dumplings can be prepared up to 3 days prior to serving.

To heat and serve, sauté with stir fry vegetables, about 5-7 per person

SESAME SOY GLAZE: In a stainless steel pot, reduce sugar, soy sauce, and balsamic vinegar by half. Combine corn starch and water in small bowl to form a 'slurry'. While liquid is boiling, add sesame oil, followed by adding cornstarch slurry, continue stirring with a whisk until it thickens. Remove from heat and allow to cool. Note sauce can be made 3 days prior to serving. When reheating, use low heat and do not bring to boil or it may cause glaze to become lumpy.

TO SERVE: Preheat oven to 325 degrees. In a large roasting pan place pork and make sure meat is evenly placed not too close to each other. Cook pork until internal temperature reaches 145 degrees, approximately 20-25 minutes; or until desired internal temperature is reached. Remove pork from oven, and allow meat to rest for about 5 minutes.

Sauté stir fry vegetables and dumplings together. On plate or serving platter, place stir fry and dumplings in center. Slice pork into half-inch or 1-inch-thick slices; place meat atop vegetables; drizzle sauce over meat. Garnish pork with orange segments and sesame seeds.

COOKING TIP: Be sure to allow pork to rest after cooking, slicing or serving too fast may cause pork to be dry and lose flavor. It is better to undercook meat, rather than to overcook it.

Drazil

Drazil (lizard backward) has an eclectic, seasonally changing menu with a little something for everyone. The first priority is good, tasty food. The second is food that is purchased, stored, cooked, and prepared in the most nutritious way possible.

There is outstanding vegetarian and vegan fare, as well as delicious organic steak, chicken and wild fish on the menu.

It's real food, done right. The portabella mushroom appetizer is a gorgeous herb-marinated mushroom cap, grilled and served over a white bean ragout, or stew studded with chunks of garlic, onion, celery and car-rot and colored with kernels of corn, pieces of broccoli di rabe and roasted red peppers.

Drazil's signature fish cakes are served with three sauces and the all-time-best carrot ba-sil mashed potatoes. Quench your thirst with some unusual and tasty concoctions, in-cluding one that combines carrot and apple juice and a punch of ginger flavor. Desserts are sugar-free, but every bit as sweet. Some samples—creamy tofu cheese cake or tasty fruit cup drizzled with spicy fruit sauce.

Come on in!

Address:
6666 Black Horse Pike
Egg Harbor Township

Phone:
609-677-8829

Web:
www.drazilrestaurant.com

Signature Fish Cakes

Wild Pollock Fish Cakes Served Over Greens

Ingredients / Serves 4

pound skinless white fish fillet – Pollock, Red
  Fish, or any firm white fish will do
tablespoons chopped parsley
tablespoon thyme
½ tablespoon tarragon
ounces chopped chive or scallion
(all herbs preferably fresh)
tablespoon lemon juice
tablespoons roasted red bell pepper
tablespoons carrot
½ teaspoon mustard
tablespoons high quality vegetarian
  mayonnaise
tablespoon flour

Note: Substitutions may be made for mayo/
flour combination such as a few ounces of
mashed potatoes, ground rice, etc.

Poach fish fillets until white all the way through. You can use wine, beer, herbs, lemon, but water works just fine. Strain and cool fish. Finely chop all vegetables and herbs. After fish is cool combine with remaining ingredients. Salt and pepper to taste. Toss lightly to thoroughly combine all ingredients. Refrigerate for at least one hour. Form into four hamburger sized patties. Pan sauté over medium heat in extra virgin olive oil. Five minutes each side. Fish is already cooked, this is just to heat through. May use tartar or any favorite sauce. Serve as you wish—in a sandwich with a beer or over a salad with wine.

Dune

Dune has a laid-back, unpretentious ambiance, with a corrugated tin wall and burlap on every table. It is a motif drawn from owner Nick Weinstein's time spent in the Caribbean. Dozens of black and white images of life at the shore cover the walls.

Here, diners expect and find quality and service, comfort food with elegance and a sophisticated and inventive menu. Chef Jason Hanin is not afraid to experiment.

Seafood arrives fresh daily and fish, much of it caught in local waters, features prominently on the menu. Seared skate wing is served with herb gnocchi, asparagus, wild mushrooms and hazelnut brown butter.

Everything is made in-house, including such refreshing finishers as banana or black grape sorbet and the decadent flourless chocolate cake.

Come on in!

Address:
9510 Ventnor Avenue
Margate

Phone:
609-487-7450

Web:
www.dunerestaurant.com

Fillet Of Black Sea Bass

With A Fig, Green Bean, Crispy Pork Belly & Red Onion Salad, Soy Citrus Vinaigrette

Ingredients / Serves 1

6 ounce fillet of black bass

pinch sea salt (fleur de sel)

2 ounces blended oil (canola, corn, etc.)

SALAD

1 fresh fig

1 orange segmented

6 french green beans

½ ounce red onion slices

1 teaspoon scallions

1 teaspoon cucumber, small diced

1 teaspoon asparagus, peeled and diced

PORK BELLY

1 pound fresh pork belly (buy at Asian market
  or a good butcher)

salt

pepper

2 cups chicken broth

2 tablespoons maple syrup

1 tablespoon extra virgin olive oil

VINAIGRETTE

1 cup blended oil

⅓ cup lite soy sauce

¼ cup lemon juice

1 teaspoon sugar or honey

Take pork belly and season it good with salt and pepper, all sides. Then take the maple syrup and olive oil and rub it all over the pork belly. Place the pork in a baking dish, skin side up and add chicken broth so it comes about 1/3 the way up the pork. Next place the dish in the oven and cook at 250 degrees for about 4-5 hours. (Every oven is calibrated different so be sure to check the meat every so often.) When it is finished remove and cool. Then slice a small piece and reheat for about 2 minutes.

Next make the vinaigrette, mix all the ingredients in the blender and then let it sit. Please taste; if you need to readjust the seasoning do so. This is a broken vinaigrette so don't worry that it looks separated.

Next place a pot of water on the stove with about 2 tablespoons of salt and then bring to a boil. Next to the stove set up a bowl with ice and water, this is to stop the cooking of the vegetables.

Take green beans and pick the one end, then place in the boiling water for about 2 minutes, use your judgment, this is not an exact science. Then remove green beans and place them in the ice bath. They should still have some firmness when you bite into them. Set them aside once they are cool and remove from water.

Next take the asparagus and peel the stalk, then cut off the hard bottoms and discard, next cut off the pretty tops. Now with the stalk, take a knife and small dice the whole thing. Once you have all the stalks diced, place them in the boiling water, about 1 min, then shock in the ice water, do the same with the asparagus tops.

Next take an orange and segment it, cut off both ends, then take your knife and cut the skin off just like if you were using a peeler. Then cut out the segments, be careful of the seeds.

Then take the onion, peel it then cut in half and begin to slice it (remember you only need a few slices.)

Then cut the scallions as thin as you can, be mindful and watch your finger, just cut slow and keep your eyes on what you are doing!

Finally take the fig and cut it into 4 or 6 segments.

Take the fish fillet and dry it off very well, then flip so skin side is facing up, then take your knife and scrape it across the skin (like squeegying a car window). What you are doing is taking all the unwanted moisture and removing it from the skin. We do this so it does not stick to the pan. You do not want to cut the skin, just scrape it 5-6 times. Wipe the knife after each scrape.

Next make your salad, with all the vegetables, fruit, and 1-2 oz slice of pork belly that you reheated, toss with a tbs (more or less) of the vinaigrette, and set aside. This is a room temperature salad.

Put the oven on 400 degrees, and then get a frying pan ready. Put the pan on the stove and turn the heat on high, let the pan get very hot. Then add the oil, take the fish fillet and season with just salt (pepper will overpower the delicate bass) when the oil begins to show a little smoke gently and slowly lay the fish skin side down in the pan, do this by holding the fish at the end, and placing the opposite end in the pan and slowly adding the rest away from your body. There should be enough oil to cover the entire bottom of the fish. (If the pan and oil are hot the fish will not absorb any oil at all) cook for about 4 minutes or until you see browning on the sides. Then take a small piece of butter and put it on top of the fillet and place the whole pan in the oven for about 2-3 minutes or until the top is no longer translucent.

Remove from oven and use a spatula and pat off excess moisture. Then place the salad in a bowl and put the fish on top. Drizzle with a little extra vinaigrette and serve.

COOKING TIP: The key to sautéing any type of fillet fish is making sure that the pan is very hot before adding oil. Once the oil begins to lightly smoke, add your fish. Lightly shake the pan to ensure that the fish is not sticking to the pan.

WINE PAIRING: Any type of California style chardonnay, preferably something aged in steel.

East Bay Crab & Grille

For a taste of the sea just a little bit inland, East Bay Crab & Grille is a sure bet. You'll practically smell the salt air when you enter the dining room decorated with the stuff of sailors' dreams—fish tanks, fish nets, diving gear, and lighthouse photos.

East Bay has a varied menu with steaks, ribs and veal dishes. But the real star is the crab, with several different varieties prepared many different ways.

Blue claws are cooked Maryland style. Alaskan snow crab legs, dungeness crab legs and colossal Alaskan king crab legs are enjoyed by the pound or all-you-can-eat.

Crabmeat is the star in cakes, bisques, and steamed in the shell, served with drawn butter and a squeeze of lemon. Finish off your meal with any of their homemade treats like Chef Bob's bread pudding, carrot cake cup cakes or their signature dessert, triple chocolate mousse cake, from Pastry Chef Joan.

Come on in!

Address:
6701 Black Horse Pike
Egg Harbor Township

Phone:
609-272-7721

Web:
www.eastbaycrab.com

Shrimp Cakes

Ingredients / Serves 4

2 pounds shrimp, Big shrimp are the best because of their flavor. (Do not use tiger shrimp.)

2 large eggs

4 tablespoons real mayonnaise

1 tablespoon juice of a fresh lemon

1 tablespoon dry mustard

1 tablespoon Old Bay

1 tablespoon Worcestershire sauce

Tabasco

6 tablespoons Panko bread crumbs (Japanese style bread crumbs)

3 tablespoons flour

Peel and devein shrimp and then cut into ½" pieces

In a mixing bowl place eggs, mayo, lemon juice, dry mustard, Old Bay, Worcestershire sauce, a dash of Tabasco until smooth, (for more spice, add a few extra dashes of Tabasco or a pinch of cayenne pepper).

In a separate mixing bowl add shrimp and flour. Coat all the shrimp well then add the above mixture and fold everything together.

Add the Panko bread crumbs and mix well.

On a baking sheet either with baking paper or sprayed with PAM, scoop out eight four-ounce balls of the shrimp mixture and then hand form your shrimp cakes, just like you would for crab cakes.

Once formed, place back on the baking sheet and bake for 8 minutes in a 350 degree preheated oven. Rotate after 4 minutes to be sure all the cakes are cooked evenly.

DRINK PAIRING: Any Chardonnay, in particular Saint Francis, Sonoma or Kendall Jackson. As for the beer, definitely Blue Moon Belgian White Wheat Ale.

TIPS: To stop bacon from curling in the pan, dip it into cold water before frying.

Instead of throwing out leftover wine, freeze it into cubes for future use in casseroles and sauces.

Microwave a lemon for 15 seconds and double the juice you get before squeezing.

Always gather everything your recipe calls for and prep and pre-measure as much as you can before you start cooking.

The Ebbitt Room at the Virginia

The Ebbitt Room at the Virginia serves innovative American cuisine in a classic setting. Signature red banquettes and dramatic chandeliers provide a warm, timeless atmosphere.

Executive Chef Andrew J. Carthy offers an intriguing menu and executes each dish as an individual work of art.

Chilled East Coast oysters with "iced champagne"—six small, meaty and sweet oysters with a dollop of cream and a spoonful of American caviar with, yes, frozen champagne shaved on top.

Sautéed sea bass with foie gras, truffle mashed potatoes, leeks and balsamic reduction and pistachio dusted local scallops with scallion-crab barley and tomato marmalade are two menu stars.

After dessert, choose something from the after-dinner drink menu and enjoy it in front of the fireplace.

Come on in!

Address:
25 Jackson Street
Cape May

Phone:
609-884-5700

Web:
www.virginiahotel.com

Pistachio Dusted Local Scallops

Pistachio Dusted Local Scallops with Scallion-Crab Barley and Tomato Marmalade

Ingredients / Serves 4

TOMATO MARMALADE

plum tomatoes, seeded and diced

oranges, zested and juiced

½ cup sugar

½ cup orange juice

½ cup white balsamic vinegar

BARLEY

cup pearl barley, washed

cup chicken stock

½ pound Maryland blue crab

4 scallions, sliced on bias

2 tablespoons butter

Salt and pepper to taste

TOASTED BUTTER VINAIGRETTE

¼ pound unsalted butter

cup balsamic vinegar

1 tablespoon olive oil

Salt and pepper to taste

ASSEMBLY

16 large dry scallops

cup micro greens (beet tops, mache, cress, basil, or any small greens)

4 tablespoons lemon oil

3 tablespoons chopped pistachios

RUB RECIPE

cup sugar

½ cup coarse sea salt

½ teaspoon cayenne powder

½ cup olive oil

TOMATO MARMALADE: In a heavy bottom saucepot over medium heat cook the tomatoes until slightly softened, add the sugar, orange zest, orange juice and balsamic vinegar and cook until syrupy, lower the heat and continue to cook until thick and jammy. Set aside until needed.

BARLEY: Place barley in a large saucepot and cover with water. Bring to a boil, lower heat to medium and simmer until tender. Strain and return to pot with chicken stock and scallions. Cook on medium heat a further 1-2minutes until stock is almost absorbed. Lower heat and gently stir in crab and butter until the crab is warmed. Do not cook the crab too long or it will begin to shred. Season to taste and keep warm.

TOASTED BUTTER VINAIGRETTE: Toast half of the butter in a heavy bottom pan until browned. Place in a blender with the balsamic. On low add the remaining butter a little at a time until fully incorporated. Add the oil and season to taste. Keep at room temperature until needed.

ASSEMBLY: Season scallops with salt and pepper and sear on high heat until golden and caramelized. Turn scallops and top with the chopped pistachios and move to a 375 degree oven for 1-2 minutes until rare in the center.

Spoon the crab and barley mixture into the center of four large dinner plates. Place 4 scallops in a row on top of barley, leaving a small gap between each. Spoon the tomato marmalade between each scallop. Toss micro greens with lemon oil and place on top of scallops. Spoon toasted butter vinaigrette around plates.

WINE: Chef Andy Carthy says that the perfect wine to complement the scallop dish should be medium-bodied with a good balance of fruit and acid to pick up on the natural sweetness of the scallops and the zest and acid of the tomato marmalade.

His suggested wines–a Gruner Veltliner from Austria, such as:
- Nigl, Gruner Veltliner, Seftenberg Kremstal 2006
- Domaine Girard, Sancerre, Loire 2006
- Morgan Chardonnay, Metallico, Monterey County 2005

COOKING TIP: Use a sugar based rub to make perfectly grilled steaks. The sugar in the recipe allows the meat to caramelize and char quickly without having to leave on the grill a long time and increase the chances of burning or over-cooking. The added benefit is that the rub seals in the juices and maximizes the flavor.

Girasole Ristorante and Lounge

Vibrancy and vitality are what you first notice about Girasole Ristorante. The décor is lively and sleekly sophisticated. The cuisine is sophisticated Italian, reminiscent of the Tuscan region. The name means "sunflower." A flickering brick oven and folds of fabric in a tented effect on the ceilings add to the warmth.

Sample pizza choices from the oven, with toppings like artichoke and truffled oil. An extensive tasting menu offers a little of many dishes, such as Octopus with Cherry Tomatoes, Black Olives and Rosemary. Carpaccios of the meat and fish variety also are great starters. Antipasti, salads and home-made pastas don't miss. And homemade tiramisu is a pretty piece of cocoa-dusted, coffee-soaked confection, with light mascarpone and cake layers.

Come on in!

Address:
3108 Pacific Avenue
Atlantic City

Phone:
609-345-5554

Web:
www.girasoleac.com

Bruschetta Di Mare

Ingredients / Serves 2

 clove of garlic, chopped
.5 ounces extra virgin olive oil
.5 ounces sundried tomatoes
4 ounces fish stock
 ounces fresh squid
 ounces octopus
 clams
 shrimp
 slices toasted bread

Sauté garlic, olive oil, sundried tomatoes, and fish stock for 4 minutes

Add the squid, octopus, clams, and shrimp.

Garnish with two slices of toasted bread on the side.

Total cooking time is 15 minutes

COOKING TIP: Always use extra virgin olive oil, sea salt, and fresh herbs (in that order).

WINE: White wine, Lacryma Christi Del Vesuvio

JP Prime

A classic steakhouse with a contemporary bar, JP Prime is an oasis of civilization, with striped suede-like banquettes and cowhide-backed leather chairs. It has all the cuts a steak-lover craves, plus plenty of seafood.

Interesting starters include Cape May calamari, piled high on the plate with an apple cider dipping sauce, sweet with honey and hot with red pepper flakes. Lobster popcorn is beer-battered chunks of deep-fried lobster with a crust.

The chipotle hanger steak can only be described as gorgeous. Marinated with dried and smoked jalapeno peppers and red wine, served with a sweet-sour balsamic reduction.

The giant baked potatoes are shipped in special from the West and prepared to a perfectly seasoned state of potato-Zen. Or try sautéed spinach, fresh baby leaves quickly heated in oil, or pesto flavored onion rings served covered with crisp Japanese breadcrumbs.

Come on in!

Address:
206 Olde New Jersey Avenue
North Wildwood

Phone:
609-729-4141

Web:
www.jpprime.com

Salmon Fillet

Scottish Salmon Fillet with Edamame Beans, Lemon, Soy, and Crisp Ginger

Ingredients / Serves 4

(4) 8 ounce Scottish salmon fillets (skin off or on)
Kosher salt and white pepper to taste
¾ cup shelled edamame beans

LEMON SOY
½ cup light soy sauce
1¼ cup rice wine vinegar
½ cup granulated sugar
¼ cup fresh lemon juice
⅓ cup Water

CRISPY GINGER
1" piece of peeled ginger
¾ cup salad oil (you can substitute other neutral oil's).
Shichimi spice.

Going with the grain, slice ginger into long strips. Ginger should be almost transparent. Julienne into very thin strips and reserve. Heat ¼ of the salad oil in a small pot or pan to medium heat. Add ginger carefully, and simmer till light golden brown in color. (Test a few strips of ginger and adjust the temperature of the oil if needed). Strain ginger and put aside. Tip: Reserve oil for other uses. Season with Shichimi spice.

Combine all ingredients to make lemon soy, making sure that the sugar is dissolved. Reserve

Preheat oven to 375 degrees. Season salmon fillets and heat oil in a sauté pan till just about smoking. Sauté salmon fillets for about a minute on both sides and put in oven. Cook for 3 minutes or until desired temperature.

Blanch edamame beans in salted boiling water for about a minute and strain. Divide edamame beans on warm plates or shallow bowls. Lay salmon in center and spoon on lemon soy. Dust salmon with Shichimi spice and garnish with crispy ginger.

WINE: Kim Crawford Sauvignon Blanc.

Karen and Rei's

Chef Karen Nelson and her husband, Rei Prabhakar, have brought new meaning to the term "homemade." From bread to dessert, everything you eat in the intimate dining room at Karen and Rei's has been made here, in a gleaming stainless steel kitchen.

Preparations are contemporary American, often blending three or more influences in one dish. Filet satay appetizer is soy-marinated beef tenderloin cooked rare and served on skewers with peanut sauce. Salads such as baked hazelnut-encrusted brie nestled in baby field lettuces are enough to share, but you might not want to. There are classics such as Maryland crabcakes, as well as eclectic offerings, such as tamarind glazed venison.

Decadent banana chocolate fudge cheesecake is a layer of dark chocolate brownie topped with feathery banana flavored cheesecake crowned with caramel, pecans and a thick chocolate ganache, and, of course, fresh whipped cream.

Come on in!

Address:
1882 Route 9 North
Clermont

Phone:
609-624-8205

Web:
www.karenandrei.com

Shrimp de Provence

Ingredients

32 medium to large shrimp, peel and devein, sauté or grill

RISOTTO
1 tablespoon butter or olive oil
1 tablespoon garlic, chopped
1 onion, diced
2 cups mushrooms, assorted, trimmed and cleaned
2 cups Arborio rice
2-6 cups water or chicken stock or shrimp stock
Salt and freshly ground pepper to taste
2 cups Fontina, grated or small diced

PESTO CREAM
1 bunch basil, picked, cleaned and dried
1 teaspoon garlic, chopped
½ cup pine nuts
4 ounces extra virgin olive oil
4 ounces heavy cream
Salt and pepper to taste

RISOTTO: In a large sauté pan, melt butter and sauté garlic and onions. Add mushrooms, cook until wilted. Add rice and stir until rice becomes a chalky color toward the center. Add one cup of water at a time, stirring continuously until water is absorbed. Cook over medium heat until rice is cooked but not mushy. Remove from heat and stir in Fontina and season.

PESTO CREAM: In a food processor add all ingredients except heavy cream and mix until smooth. In a sauté pan, add pesto, lightly cook, then add the heavy cream and seasoning.

To assemble, spoon risotto into individual bowls, ring the risotto with cooked shrimp and drizzle with pesto cream.

Knife and Fork Inn

The legendary Knife and Fork Inn is a revelation. The inn has been around since 1912 and recently was restored to its original glamour and grandeur.

The transformation recaptures the look and feel of the building's Prohibition-era roots, including rich mahogany millwork, hand-painted ceilings, a sweeping staircase and balcony and lushly appointed dining rooms.

In the main dining room, find pendant lighting, tufted burgundy leather banquette seating, leaded etched glass windows and trompe l'oeil bricks on the vaulted ceiling.

Steaks and seafood are prepared on a wood-fired grill. The cuisine is complemented by the 10,000 bottle wine "cellar" on the third floor.

Among the standout dishes – mini Kobe burgers appetizer. Each medium rare burger is topped separately. Lobster thermidor is a rich, tried-and-true favorite.

Come on in!

Address:
Atlantic and Pacific avenues
Atlantic City

Phone:
609-344-1133

Web:
www.knifeandforkinn.com

Lobster Thermidor

Classic Recipe, Fresh Lobster Meat Sautéed in a Sherry, Wild Mushroom, Tarragon Cream, Finished in the Broiler with Bernaise Sauce

Ingredients / Serves 4

4 two-pound lobsters
2 tablespoons unsalted butter
¼ bunch tarragon
1 minced peeled shallot
6 sliced crimini mushrooms
1 leek, halved lengthwise, sliced ¼ inch (green and root discarded)
2 fluid ounces sherry wine
1 tablespoon Dijon mustard
½ cup heavy cream
kosher salt
ground white pepper
4 ounces bernaise

Submerge lobster in boiling water for four minutes, remove from pot and submerge in ice bath. When cool, remove claws and knuckles; remove meat from shell and cut into large pieces. Split body of lobster lengthwise down the center of the back (Be careful not to cut all the way through, you want to use the shell to serve the finished product in.) Spread body and tail apart, remove tail meat and cut into the same size pieces as claw and knuckle meat, rinse out cavity and set shell aside.

Sweat shallots and leeks in butter until slightly translucent. Add tarragon and mushrooms and sweat until wilted and moisture is released. Add lobster meat, sauté for one minute. Add sherry off of flame; flambé. Stir in Dijon, add heavy cream. Adjust salt and pepper to taste. On sheet pan, spoon the meat and sauce mixture into the cavity (body and tail) of lobster; drizzle remaining sauce on top.

Top each lobster with 1 ounce of Bernaise Sauce – evenly spread over each. Place in 350 degree oven for 5 minutes or under broiler for 40 seconds, until Bernaise is slightly browned.

WINE: Ferrari-Carano Reserve Chardonnay. This full bodied white, with almond characteristics and a warm, toasty oak finish, complements and enhances the rich flavors and textures of the Lobster Thermidor.

COOKING TIP: Always use kosher salt in place of table salt when cooking. It has a better flavor and the coarser texture allows the cook to control the amount used and taste achieved.

La Spiaggia

La Spiaggia – "the beach" in Italian – is an apt name for this quiet, classy restaurant serving northern Italian cuisine prepared with high accomplishment and style.

Chef Daniel Stragapede, co-owner with his brother, Mark, uses fresh ingredients to create dishes that appeal to the eye as well as the palate in this Mediterranean style ristorante. Zuppa di clams, either red or white, are local littleneck clams served in a broth you'll want to eat with a spoon. Chilean sea bass with tomato, fennel and saffron broth is a favorite special.

Excellent desserts include torta di anni, a

molten chocolate cake and a piped rosette of white chocolate ganache with stripes of chocolate and raspberry sauce on the plate.

Come on in!

Address:
357 W. Eighth Street
Ship Bottom

Phone:
609-494-4343

Web:
www.laspiaggialbi.com

Chilean Sea Bass

Chilean Sea Bass with Tomato, Fennel & Saffron Broth

Ingredients / Serves 4

6–8 ounce pieces of Chilean sea bass
2 dozen each littleneck clams and mussels
1 tablespoon sliced garlic
2 tablespoons canola oil
2 medium fennel bulbs, julienne
1 medium yellow onion, julienne
1 teaspoon ginger, chopped
1 cup white wine and 12 threads of saffron
 (combine and steep)
1–16 ounce can diced tomatoes in juice
1 cup clam broth
1 bay leaf
Salt and pepper to taste

In medium sauce pan, heat oil and garlic for 1 minute.

Add onion and fennel, cook until onion is translucent.

Add wine and saffron mixture. Add bay leaf. Continue to cook until wine reduces by half.

Add tomatoes, ginger, and broth; simmer 15 to 20 minutes.

Preheat oven to 375°.

Place fish, clams, mussels and sauce in oven-proof covered pan.

Bake 15 to 20 minutes or until shellfish open.

Place in bowl with sauce.

TIP: Fresh ginger can easily be peeled with a tablespoon.

WINE: 2006 Raymond Sauvignon Blanc Reserve.

Laguna Grill & Martini Bar

There's something special about drinking exotic martinis and tropical cocktails and enjoying delicious food, all while overlooking the gorgeous ocean.

Laguna Grill & Martini Bar offers all this and more — breakfast, lunch, dinner, a light tavern menu and pre-theater offerings. All tables have a great ocean view. Or sit on the open beachside deck.

Enter through beautiful curved mosaic walls to find a unique ambience. Mix in excellent service with impressive attention to detail and lively entertainment for a memorable dining experience.

Very fresh seafood is a hallmark. Pan-seared diver scallops are served with beluga lentils, spinach, and roasted tomatoes in a beurre-blanc sauce. Dishes of steak, pork, chicken, pasta, and house-made desserts — warm chocolate torte and vanilla crème brulee — are magnificent.

Come on in!

Address:
1400 Ocean Avenue
Brigantine

Phone:
609-266-7731

Web:
www.lagunagrill.com

Portuguese Clay Pot Red Snapper

An Amazing Seafood Delight!

ounce red snapper fillet

white water mussels

cup roasted plum tomato sauce or your
  favorite red sauce

cup fish or chicken stock

whole fingerling potatoes (sliced lengthwise)

green beans

kalamata olives

fried long hot pepper

large garlic clove, sliced

tablespoon chopped cilantro and a
  tablespoon chopped basil

alt and pepper to taste

fried, sliced plantain for garnish

Place olive oil and garlic in a 10-inch sauté pan. When garlic browns, add mussels and red snapper. Sauté for 1 to 2 minutes. Add tomato sauce, fish or chicken stock, potatoes, green beans, kalamata olives, cilantro, basil, salt & pepper. Simmer for approximately 10 minutes. Place the contents into a clay pot, garnish with long pepper and crisp plantain.

WINE: White: Sonoma Cutrer Chardonnay, Russian River.
        Red: Mark West Pinot Noir, California

COOKING TIP: Save leftover chopped herbs by freezing them. Make sure they are washed and dried completely on a paper towel. The cubes come in handy for throwing in a sauce or stew.

Los Amigos

Contemporary southwestern and Mexican border fare is in abundance at the cozy Los Amigos Mexican Restaurant and Bar. In addition to the favorite burritos and quesadillas, find an array of interesting specialties, such as grilled fish and filet mignon prepared with spice and herb rubs, served sizzling hot.

Start off with just-fried-to-perfection thin tortilla chips dipped in wonderful guacamole, mashed avocados with bits of onion, tomatoes and loads of cilantro.

Fresh, colorful ingredients pop in dishes like southwest crab cakes and shrimp dinner enhanced with jalapeno, cholula hot sauce and mild southwest tartar sauce, and filet-mignon tacos.

Come on in!

Address:
1926 Atlantic Avenue
Atlantic City

Phone:
609-344-2293

Web:
www.losamigosrest.com

Mescalero Mussels

Black Mussels with a Roasted Garlic and Red Hot Pasilla Chili Broth

Ingredients / Serves 4

MUSSELS

dozen cleaned mussels
ounces oil
tablespoon minced garlic
cup tequila
cup Frank's hot sauce
cup pico de gallo
ounces chicken stock
tablespoons chopped cilantro
slices of thick bread
lime cut into 8 wedges
teaspoon pico de gallo

PICO DE GALLO

diced tomatoes
small diced onion
minced jalapeno to taste
cup chopped cilantro to taste
cup lime juice to taste
lt to taste

DON JULIO POMEGRANATE MARGARITA

ounces Don Julio Blanco Tequila
ounces Grand Marnier
ounces fresh squeezed lime juice
ounces pomegranate juice
sher salt (to rim the glass)

Heat oil in a large sauté pan.

Add mussels and garlic, cook over high heat for 2 minutes.

Take pan off the heat source, add the tequila and flame.

When the alcohol has burned off, add hot sauce and incorporate well.

Add chicken broth, pico de gallo and cilantro, cover.

Cook over high heat for 5 minuets or until mussels open.

Pour into large bowl and serve with lime wedges, the toasted bread and more pico de gallo.

COOKING TIPS: Cook and macerate your favorite fruits when in season. Blend them up to a smooth puree, put in an ice cube tray and freeze. Whenever you have guests over for margaritas, you can blend the cubes with your margarita ingredients to make your favorite fruit margarita.

Mad Batter

A Cape May tradition since 1975, the Mad Batter offer diners a chance to enjoy a wonderful meal on a covered European-style front porch, on a secluded garden terrace or in a skylit dining room.

Breakfast, lunch or dinner is a special occasion in this beautifully restored Victorian era villa. For breakfast, try something unique — the Morgan Rostie Omelet with super lump crabmeat, sun-dried tomatoes, fried potatoes and herbs, and Swiss cheese.

At lunch, the BALT sandwich is a twist on an old favorite. Peppered bacon, avocado, green leaf lettuce and tomato served on bri-oche toast with lobster Louis dressing and sweet potato fries.

Delicious clam chowder is rich with the taste of slab bacon, onions, a touch of saffron, tender clams, and heavy cream.

Try the fresh taste of Chilean sea bass marinated in Mirin, a Japanese rice wine, and served with jasmine rice, steamed baby bok choy, and sweet soy sauce. Save room for a homemade dessert such as decadent chocolate lava cake or Irish crème brulee.

Come on in!

Address:
19 Jackson Street
Cape May

Phone:
609-884-5970

Web:
www.madbatter.com

Sautéed Sea Scallops

Pan Sautéed Sea Scallops with Pumpkin Raviolis and Sage Pecan Butter

Ingredients / Serves 4

- 1 pound jumbo sea scallops, about 16
- 12 pumpkin raviolis, cooked according to package directions and cooled
- 8 ounces chanterelle mushrooms, cleaned and sliced
- 8 ounces crimini mushrooms, cleaned and sliced
- ½ bunch sage, julienned
- 3 ounces chopped pecans
- 2 ounces clarified butter
- 4 ounces whole butter

Season scallops with salt and pepper.

In large sauté pan, heat clarified butter.

Sear scallops on one side, turn and lightly brown on other side, remove from pan. Drain butter from pan, then add in whole butter, mushrooms, and ravioli. Toss until raviolis are slightly brown and mushrooms are soft.

Add in sage and pecans, toss until butter is nicely brown.

Arrange raviolis and scallops on plate, pour remaining butter and nuts on top.

COOKING TIP: To cook perfect rice, always rinse the rice before cooking. Use 1 ½ – 2 cups of water for 1 cup of rice. Longer grain rice requires more water than shorter grain. To flavor the rice, use fresh herbs in the water or cook with broth. Boil rice for 12 minutes until the liquid is absorbed and let the pot rest with the lid on for at least 5 minutes.

Manna

Walk into Manna and you feel like one of the family. Warmth, friendliness and great service are part of the experience. "Feed your body, nourish your soul" is the mantra here.

The dining room is inviting, with maple flooring, mahogany tables and pendant lighting. There is seating on the sidewalk in addition to the cozy dining room.

Cuisine is new American, recognizable food done in a new way. The menu changes seasonally. Summertime, palate pleasers are appetizers of jumbo lump crab and tomato risotto and wasabi two-pepper shrimp. Paella, a perennial favorite, is brimming with jumbo shrimp, lump crab, clams, fish, chicken, chorizo, rice, saffron, and tomato.

Antipasto feeds two with its variety of Italian meats, sharp provolone, olive salad, roasted peppers, artichokes, asparagus, and anchovies.

Dessert is a family affair, all made in-house. Maple crème brulee, pecan pie and "chocolate degustation" – mousse, rich velvety chocolate cake, bittersweet hot chocolate and raspberry-white chocolate ganache — are among the stars.

Come on in!

Address:
8409 Ventnor Avenue
Margate

Phone:
609-822-7722

Web:
www.mannaventnor.com

Paella "Our Way"

Ingredients / Serves 1

½ cup raw, peeled and chopped chorizo (spicy Spanish sausage)

10 clams

5 large shrimp, peeled and deveined

½ cup cooked and picked chicken thighs

1 teaspoon chopped garlic

½ teaspoon saffron

2 cups cooked arborio rice (packed)

½ cup plum tomatoes, peeled and julienned

½ cup white wine

1 cup clam juice or shell fish stock (more if necessary)

salt and pepper

½ cup jumbo lump crab

12" heavy bottom sauté pan or paella pan with lid

Place sauté pan or paella pan on medium heat. Brown chorizo. Drain some fat. Add clams, shrimp, chicken, garlic, and saffron. Cover for two minutes, allowing ingredients to steam. Add cooked rice, tomatoes, white wine, and stock. Season with salt and pepper. Cover and cook until just about all liquid is absorbed and clams are open. Add more stock if too dry. Add crab and stir. Serve hot.

WINE: If red is desired, chef recommends Rioja Reserve. If white is preferred, enjoy a Rueda.

COOKING TIP: To extend the life of asparagus place the ends in water and refrigerate.

Pacific Grill

Pacific Grill achieves a surf casual atmosphere with warm woods, soft lighting, plush seating and a color scheme of tan and light green. Add to that a menu of comfortable American cuisine that gives a twist to familiar items and you have a recipe for success.

Everything here is fresh, with seafood taking center stage. Take the crispy fried calamari with Kalamata and nicoise olives, Jersey tomatoes, capers and poblano peppers, instead of traditional marinara sauce. Ahi tuna is flown in from Honolulu three times a week and may be served with pepper-coriander crust, Asian noodle salad, soy-mirin glace and wasabi aioli. Seared dayboat scallops with lobster risotto, baby spinach, and olive oil poached tomato also wow.

House-made desserts include specialty ice creams like rum raisin and banana. Profiteroles with chocolate sauce and vanilla ice cream are to die for.

Come on in!

Address:
4801 Pacific Avenue
Wildwood

Phone:
609-523-1800

Web:
www.pacificgrillwildwood.com

Pacific Grill Grouper

Seared Grouper with Verjus Sauce, Wilted Escarole, and Stone-Ground Grits

Ingredients / Serves 4

GROUPER

4 6-8 ounce pieces of grouper, cleaned, boned and patted dry

2 tablespoons of grape seed oil

Salt and pepper to taste

VERJUS SAUCE

2 tablespoons of unsalted butter

1 ½ cups of Verjus (unripened/ unfermented grape juice from wine grapes found in specialty markets)

1 tablespoon of chopped parsley

1 tablespoon of chopped chives

½ tablespoon of minced garlic

½ tablespoon of minced shallots

ESCAROLE

½ lemon

1 head of escarole, cleaned and cut into 1-inch pieces

4 slices of bacon (rendered and crisp)

1 tablespoon of caramelized Spanish onions

2 tablespoons of olive oil

1 tablespoon of minced garlic

Salt and pepper to taste

GRITS

2 cups of stone-ground grits

¼ cup of milk

¼ cup of chicken stock

Preheat oven to 300 degrees Fahrenheit.

Season grouper on both sides with salt and pepper then sear in a very hot pan with grape seed oil until one side is golden brown and has developed a crust. Remove the fish from the pan and place crust side up on a baking sheet for 5-10 minutes depending on thickness.

For the verjus sauce, reduce the verjus to ¼ then add all other ingredients except butter. Season the sauce with salt and pepper then whisk in butter to emulsify.

WINE: Vouvray

COOKING TIP: Always dry all seafood before searing. The food is easier to handle and there is less splatter. Also, put a little butter in with your oil when searing to get a perfect brown coating.

Peregrines'

Peregrines' is the only boutique gourmet restaurant in an Atlantic City casino. With just 52 seats – including a private study with a table for 10 – Peregrines' sets the standard for other gourmet rooms in the city.

Named for the peregrine falcons that have made their home on the ledge of the Atlantic City Hilton, Peregrines' offers an upscale continental experience focusing on seafood. It's the type of place where you receive an amuse-bouche to start, truffles after dessert, and roses for the ladies when exiting.

Focusing on service and quality ingredients, Peregrines' is the only Atlantic City restaurant to receive a "Five-Star" rating by the American Academy of Restaurant & Hospitality Sciences.

With a warm, quiet, European setting that features beautiful draperies, marble and plush, semi-private banquettes, the main attraction is the menu as Chef Robert LaBoy creates a balance of classic and modern cuisine.

There's something for everyone on Peregrines' menu; all of it has a Peregrines' touch. Peregrines' lump crabmeat margarita is served with key lime and tequila sorbet and a cucumber salad. The quesadilla features lobster with manchego cheese, mango and plum tomato salsa. The Chilean sea bass is pistachio seared, sliced thin and served with slow-roasted tomatoes, midnight cauliflower puree and yellow pepper oil. And the seared filet mignon is served with a heaping pile of jumbo crabmeat in a Far Niente chardonnay cream with sweet potato gratin and roasted tomatoes.

Come on in!

Address:
Atlantic City Hilton
3400 Pacific Avenue
Atlantic City

Phone:
609-236-7870

Web:
www.hiltonac.com

Paella & Red Mole

Sautéed Maine Lobster, Shrimp, and Scallops With King Crab Paella and Red Mole

Ingredients / Serves 1

SEAFOOD

(1) 1½-pound live
    Maine lobster

2 jumbo scallops,
    cleaned

2 jumbo shrimp,
    peeled, deveined,
    tail on

2 tablespoons
    unsalted butter

¼ cup white wine

½ teaspoon fine
    sea salt

1 pinch white pepper

FOR KING CRAB PAELLA

1 cup basmati rice

2 cups fish stock

2 ounces king crab
    meat, rough chopped

1 pinch saffron threads

2 tablespoons
    unsalted butter

1 tablespoon finely
    chopped shallots

1 tablespoon
    chopped scallions

1 teaspoon fine sea salt

½ teaspoon white
    pepper

FOR RED MOLE SAUCE

1 red bell pepper,
    seeds and stem
    removed, large dice

1 yellow bell pepper,
    seeds and stem
    removed, large diced

½ small peeled
    Spanish onion,
    rough chopped

½ chipotle pepper,
    seeds removed

2 tablespoons extra
    virgin olive oil

1 teaspoon fine sea
    salt

1 tablespoon shaved
    extra bitter dark
    chocolate

Have bowl of ice water ready. Remove tail and claws from live lobster. Cook in boiling lightly salted water for 5 minutes. Remove and place in ice water immediately. Let cool completely. Then remove outer shell from lobster tail leaving tail end intact (kitchen shears work well for this task). Remove any visible vein. Remove claw meat by laying on a firm flat surface and cracking shell with the back of a French knife on both sides. Gently remove the shell, leaving the meat intact. Refrigerate until use.

RED MOLE: Sauté all ingredients EXCEPT for chocolate until softened. Let cool until just warm. Transfer into blender and puree until smooth. While still warm, add chocolate and blend well. Reserve until served.

PAELLA: Sauté shallots in 1 tablespoon of butter until translucent. Then add rice, stock, saffron, salt and pepper, and stir. Cover and lightly simmer until rice is tender. Fold in scallions and king crab. Keep warm.

Preheat oven to 340 degrees. Melt one tablespoon butter on medium heat in non-stick sauté pan. Season shrimp, scallops, and lobster tail and claw meat, and sear until lightly browned, noting that the tail should be top down. Add white wine and finish in oven for 8 minutes.

TO ASSEMBLE: First place paella onto plate slightly off center to the left. Then arrange shrimp and scallops neatly on the left side of paella. Place the lobster tail onto the paella. Cross the two pieces of claw meat in front of paella. Make a pan sauce by adding 1 tablespoon of butter to the pan and lightly stirring until thickened. Cover the seafood with the sauce. To finish, spoon small spots of the red mole onto the right side of the plate and serve. A nice accent vegetable is pencil size asparagus sautéed in shallots and butter and accented with chili threads.

COOKING TIP: Sea Salt has less sodium than table or kosher salt, so it is a better option for those on low sodium diets.

Rama Thai

A golden experience starts when you step through the doors of Rama Thai. Immerse yourself in this culture of warm and loving people with traditional Thai iced tea – a layer of sweetened condensed milk on top. Servers are friendly and beautifully attired in traditional Thai costumes of brilliant colors.

Delicious Thai fare includes a satay gai appetizer, sliced chicken marinated in coconut milk with a hint of Thai curry spice, skewered and grilled. The combination plate allows sampling stuffed chicken wings, light and airy triangles of fried tofu, spicy fish cakes, crisp calamari, and egg rolls.

Rama duck is a crisp-skinned half duck, sliced and topped with a wonderful sauce of coconut milk, red curry paste, pineapple pieces, tomato chunks and lots of Thai basil. A chef's special seafood stir fry of shrimp, squid, scallops, mussels and fish with curry paste, and crisp vegetables is sure to please.

Come on in!

Address:
3003 English Creek Avenue
Egg Harbor Township

Phone:
609-677-1004

Web:
www.ramathainj.com

Pad Thai

Ingredients / Serves 4

8 ounces Thai rice noodles
¼ cup tamarind paste
¼ cup warm water
¼ cup white sugar
4 ounces skinless, boneless chicken breast
4 ounces fried tofu
6 tablespoons roasted unsalted peanuts
3 tablespoons fish sauce
2 tablespoons white vinegar
½ cup vegetable oil
1 teaspoon chopped garlic
10 large shrimp, shelled and deveined
   (50 ounces)
2 eggs
1 cup bean sprouts
2 stems green onion, cut into 1-inch pieces
1 lime, juiced

SIDE OF DISH
¼ cup roasted chilies
1 cup fresh bean sprouts
1 lime, cut into wedges
¼ cup fresh coriander leaves
¼ cup red bell pepper, cut into strips

Soak noodles in plenty of cold water for at least 1 hour.

Combine tamarind paste with a 1/4 cup warm water in a small bowl and let soak for at least 15 minutes.

Slice the chicken into 1/4-inch strips. If you find it difficult to cut thinly through fresh meat, leave it in the freezer for 15-20 minutes to harden slightly and then slice. Reserve.

Slice the fried tofu into 3/4-inch cubes. Reserve.

Blend or process peanuts into coarse meal. Reserve.

Return to your reserved tamarind paste in its water. Mash it and transfer the mud-like mixture to a strainer set into a bowl. Mash and push with a spoon, forcing liquid to strain into the bowl. Scrape off the juice that clings to the underside of the strainer. You will have about 5 tbsp of tamarind juice. Add to it the fish sauce, sugar, and lime juice. Beat to thoroughly mix and re-serve. Discard the solids left in the strainer.

Heat oil in a wok (or large frying pan) until it is just about to smoke. Add garlic and stir, letting it cook for about 30 seconds. Add chicken and stir-fry for 1 minute. Add tofu and shrimp and stir-fry for 1 more minute. Break eggs into wok and let them fry without breaking them up for 1-2 minutes.

While eggs cook, quickly drain the noodles and then add to wok, giving them a quick fold, stir-frying for 1 minute from the bottom up. Add reserved tamarind juice, etc. (from step #6) and continue stir-frying, mixing everything together for 1-2 minutes. Your noodles will have subsided to half their original volume and softened up to al dente.

Add about 2/3 of the reserved ground peanuts and stir. Add about 2/3 of the bean sprouts and all the green onion pieces. Stir-fry for 30 seconds and take off heat.

Transfer noodles to a serving dish and sprinkle with roasted chilies. Top with the rest of the ground peanuts, the rest of the sprouts, some strips of red pepper, and fresh coriander leaves. Stick a couple of lime wedges on the side and serve immediately.

COOKING TIP: If you use too little oil, the noodles will stick and you'll have a mess in your wok.

Red Sky Café

When it comes to creating an attractive restaurant that offers delicious Southwestern cuisine, Red Sky Café owners Jeff and Greta Schwartz know what they are doing. A neon sign invites you into the colorful building. Vibrant oranges, purples and golds greet you, and wagon wheels, cacti, and even a bull's head offer a fun vibe. A separate bar has wood accents.

Signature barbecue beef, chicken and veggies are offered in burritos, chimichangas, enchiladas and more. The menu is rounded out by steaks, ribs, seafood, sandwiches and salads. Blue corn crab cakes, the chef's original recipe, and seasoned grilled fillet of grouper with fresh fruit salsa are among the tasty specialties.

Gargantuan, tasty margaritas are served in hand-blown martini glasses from Mexico.

Come on in!

Address:
Atlantic and Schellenger aves.
Wildwood

Phone:
609-522-7747

Web:
www.redskycafe.net

Greta's Favorite Grouper

Pan Grilled Fillet of Grouper with Tropical Fruit Salsa

Ingredients / Serves 4

4 teaspoons olive oil, divided
4 (8-ounce} grouper fillets

SEASONING BLEND FOR GROUPER

2 tablespoons kosher salt
2 tablespoons course ground pepper
2 tablespoons paprika
2 tablespoons fresh chopped garlic
1 tablespoon cayenne pepper
1 tablespoon dried oregano
1 tablespoon dried thyme

FRUIT SALSA

3/4 cup small diced peaches
3/4 cup small diced mango
1/2 cup small diced strawberries
1/2 cup small diced pineapples
1/4 cup small diced red onion
1 jalapeno, stemmed, seeded, and finely
    chopped
2 tablespoons freshly chopped cilantro
2 tablespoons freshly squeezed orange juice
1 tablespoon freshly squeezed lime juice
1/4 teaspoon of kosher salt
1 teaspoon honey

Combine the grouper seasoning ingredients thoroughly. In a medium stainless steel bowl combine all fruit salsa ingredients and stir to blend. Cover with plastic wrap and allow the fruit salsa to marinate for 30 minutes before serving.

FISH PREPARATION: Preheat a grill to medium. Brush both sides of the grouper with olive oil. Season the grouper on both sides with the blend. Place the fish on the grill and cook for about 3 minutes, lift the fish off the grill and turn it 45 degrees and place down on grill for another 3 minutes. This will give the grouper its score marks. Turn the fish over and cook for an additional 2 minutes or until desired doneness is reached.

Remove grouper from the grill and spoon on the fresh fruit salsa. Serve immediately.

WINE: Try a dry red wine with this dish as it complements both the fish and salsa. You also cannot go wrong with a Mexican beer with a slice of lime.

COOKING TIP: The term Mis En Place translates into "everything in its place." This means be organized, have your pans, bowls and cooking utensils ready to be used. Place your ingredients in front of you, measured and cut to spec according to the recipe. Make sure you clean up as you go.

Red Square

To dine at Red Square at the Quarter at the Tropicana Casino and Resort is to be immersed in the elegance of imperial Russia. Guests walk past the impressive statue of Lenin and through the giant, gold leaf doors to enter the plush world of Red Square's distinctly Russian ambience. Rich red velvet banquette seating abounds and distressed walls reveal old Russian icons and political propaganda.

Dine on eclectic Perestroika-inspired cuisine, including a wide selection of the world's finest caviars and a mix of French, European, Asian, and classic American flavors. Siberian nachos are wonton wrappers halved and crisply deep fried, topped with strips of smoked salmon, tobiko caviar and wasabi cream. The Kulebyaka-dilled seared fillet of salmon is served on a puff pastry with wild mushroom risotto and dill saffron beurre blanc risotto.

Famous for its private vodka lockers, Red Square keeps its vodka at subfreezing temperatures. Ladies get fur coats and gentlemen get authentic Russian army coats to wear while visiting their private vodka storage. The impressive frozen ice bar features more than 130 frozen vodkas, infusions and martinis.

Come on in!

Address:
The Quarter at the Tropicana
2801 Pacific Avenue
Atlantic City

Phone:
609-344-9100

Web:
www.chinagrillmgt.com/redsquarenj

Red Square's Tuna Tartare

Ingredients / Serves 2

8 ounces fresh diced tuna (sushi grade)
2 tablespoons toasted pine nuts
1 tablespoon chopped fresh chives
1 teaspoon black sesame seeds
1 ounce Sambal Ponzu
2 ounces wasabi crème fraiche

GARNISHES

1 each hard boiled quail egg
1 teaspoon American sturgeon caviar
Served with potato gaufrettes

SAMBAL PONZU

1 cup lite soy sauce
5 ounces cold water
1 tablespoon sambal (chili paste)
1 tablespoon fresh lime juice
1 teaspoon sesame oil

WASABI CRÈME FRAICHE

6 tablespoons wasabi powder
4 ounces cold water
10 ounces sour cream
8 ounces heavy cream

TUNA TARTARE: Mix tuna, pine nuts, sesame seeds, chives, and sambal ponzu together until all of the ingredients are blended. Using a pastry bag, paint an attractive design of wasabi crème fraiche onto your serving plate. Mold the tartare onto the plate and garnish. The tartare can be served with any type of chips or crackers.

SAMBAL PONZU: Mix all ingredients together until well blended, then strain.

WASABI CRÈME FRAICHE: First mix wasabi powder and water together to make a paste, then set aside. Then mix sour cream and heavy cream together until well blended. Last fold the wasabi paste into the cream mixture, blend until smooth.

COOKING TIP: The best way to thaw frozen meats is gradually in the refrigerator. Plan accordingly; it will maintain the quality of the food much better than any other means of thawing and it's much safer. The larger the item, the longer you should allow for it to properly thaw. The second best way is thaw it under continuous running cold water.

WINE: Saintsbury Pinot Noir.

Ri Ra Irish Pub and Restaurant

Ri Ra is an authentic Irish pub where music and merriment marry, located in The Quarter at the Tropicana Casino and Resort. It is built entirely from authentic salvage material, including the impressive bar from the notable Henry Grattan Pub in Dublin, where James Joyce used to drink and write. The name comes from "Ri-Ra agus Ruaile Buaile," a phrase translating roughly as: "devilment, good fun or any sociable activity that improves with fine food, a nice pint of Guinness or dram of Uisce Beatha (whiskey)." Liquid refreshment is very important here. So is delicious food.

Irish potato cakes are served with a savory sour cream sauce and balsamic reduction. Fish and chips is a crowd-pleaser with mushy peas mashed to the consistency of mashed potatoes. Corned beef and cabbage, as well as bangers and mash — Irish sausage served with roasted tomato, mashed potato and baked beans – are among the traditional Irish fare. And all day you can get an Irish breakfast, a proper fry up of eggs, bangers, rashers, pudding, tomato, and beans. Don't miss the Guinness ice cream.

Come on in!

Address:
2801 Pacific Avenue
Atlantic City

Phone:
609-348-8600

Web:
www.rira.com

Bantry Bay Mussels

1 pound cleaned Bantry Bay Mussels
   (substitute any black mussels)
2 ounces chopped garlic
1 ounce olive oil
1 lemon, quartered
4 ounces white wine (Sauvignon Blanc
   preferred)
3 ounces whole unsalted butter
1 bunch parsley chopped

Scrub and de-beard mussels.

Heat large sauté pan with olive oil.

Add mussels and sauté for 1 minute.

Add garlic and sauté for 30 seconds.

Deglaze pan with white wine.

Cover for 2 minutes or until mussels open.

Reduce heat, add butter and parsley, swirl in pan until melted and sauce is formed.

Season with salt and pepper.

Pour into large bowl.

Garnish with lemon wedges, chopped parsley, and crusty bread

DRINK PAIRING: The traditional drink with mussels back home is Guinness (of course, we also recommend Guinness with dessert and even breakfast).

COOKING TIP: Check the fresh mussels for live / dead state. If a mussel is partially open, gently tap the shell. If it closes the mussel is live and good. If it remains open, it is dead and should be trashed. When you get home, wash the shellfish vigorously under cold running water to remove, sand, grit and other materials from the shell.

Cook as desired until all shells open. If some of them don't open, discard them.

Sage

Lisa Savage's Sage is the epitome of contemporary elegance, more urban than shore town, without big-city pretense. Decor is simple and arty, with a soothing earth color scheme that exudes warmth.

The cuisine is uncomplicated, European style, a blend of Asian, southwestern, Mediterranean and Italian. Calamari is impeccable, served with two sauces, a light, zesty marinara and a luscious, creamy kalamata olive aioli touched with garlic. Mozzarella trio is six slices of moist cheese with three toppings – roasted cherry tomatoes, roasted red peppers, and basil pesto.

Pan-seared Mediterranean sea bass is nestled beneath sautéed tomato, scallions, kalamata olives and baby artichokes and seasoned with a fragrant white wine reduction sauce. Two signature desserts, flourless chocolate cake and banana cream pie, are flawless.

Come on in!

Address:
5206 Atlantic Avenue
Ventnor

Phone:
609-823-2110

Lisa's Zuppa

Roman Style Fish Soup/Stew

10 Plum tomatoes (cut in half vertically)
3 cloves minced garlic
5 sprigs of fresh thyme
5 stems of fresh basil
Extra virgin olive oil
Salt and pepper
4 cups shellfish or low sodium chicken stock
1 medium onion, small dice
3 cloves of garlic, sliced thin
2 tablespoons olive oil
1 tablespoon basil, chopped
4 whole lobsters cut in half and cleaned
8 pieces of 20-30 count dry packed scallops
8 pieces of jumbo shrimp
16-20 little neck clams
40 mussels, cleaned
2 cloves of garlic, sliced
2 tablespoons olive oil
1 cup of white wine
2 tablespoons chopped Italian parsley
8 pieces of garlic toast

Preheat oven to 350 degrees.

Place tomatoes on a baking sheet (you may have to slice a bit off the ends to stop them from rolling over).

First sprinkle the tops of the tomatoes with garlic, then scatter thyme and basil over them and drizzle with extra-virgin olive oil. Season with salt and pepper and cook in the oven at 350 degrees until tomatoes start to wrinkle and soften. Remove and cool.

Sauté onions and garlic until soft and they start to caramelize.

Place onions in a blender with 12 pieces of roasted tomatoes and basil. Add stock until you achieve a slightly broth consistency, put aside.

In a large pot, sauté garlic until it begins to turn golden, add lobsters and wine.

Cook until lobsters turn red and wine is almost gone. Add clams, scallops, and tomato broth and bring to a simmer, covered. When clams open add shrimp, mussels, and reserved roasted tomatoes. Continue to cook covered until mussels open. Divide shellfish into deep bowls and add tomato broth. Garnish with 2 pieces of garlic toast per person, sprinkle chopped parsley on top.

COOKING TIP: Never be intimidated by lengthy recipes with lots of steps and ingredients. Just make sure all is prepped before you start. Have everything ready and have fun with it.

WINE: My wine choice is a light red. Dolcetto d'seba Alba or Pinot Noir.

Sea Salt

True to its name, Sea Salt is about simplicity and purity in ingredients. The Asian and Mediterranean-inspired menu makes mouthwatering use of locally grown produce, fresh meat and seafood delivered daily.

Dream of dining near the blue sea as you feast on summer vegetables tossed with pistou — made by pounding basil, olive oil, garlic and sea salt in a mortar and pestle into a summery green sauce, it is the French equivalent of pesto without the cheese.

A chef's favorite is grilled hanger steak topped with chimichurri and accompanied by hand cut French fries provencal, home-made Argentinian style grilled sausage, and heirloom tomatoes and basil salad.

Sea Salt's atmosphere is that of a tiny seaside shop, with a vintage feel created by antique chairs and sideboard and paint-by-number paintings that date back to the 1940s and 1950s. Don't be surprised if Owner/Chef Lucas Manteca greets you in his white chef's coat with a plate of food.

Come on in!

Address:
8307 Third Avenue
Stone Harbor

Phone:
609-368-3302

Web:
www.seasaltstoneharbor.com

Butternut Squash Soup

THE SOUP

- 2 butternut squash, peeled, seeded and diced
- 1 Spanish onion, peeled, thin sliced
- 3 tablespoons extra virgin olive oil
- 2 bay leaves
- 1 tablespoon brown sugar
- ½ teaspoon cinnamon
- ½ teaspoon nutmeg, grated
- ¼ teaspoon all spiced, ground
- ½ teaspoon black pepper, ground
- 3 teaspoons fine salt, sea salt preferred

THE GARNISH

- 20 pieces live mussels, Prince Edward Island preferred
- ½ pound fresh crab meat, Peeky Toe crab out of Maine preferred
- 1 bunch fresh cilantro, leaves carefully picked
- 1 bunch fresh chives
- 1 bunch fresh parsley
- 1 cup unsalted pumpkin seeds
- 1 teaspoon cayenne pepper
- 1 cup fresh mango
- 1 cup golden raisins
- 1 cup creme fraiche or sour cream
- 1 cup heavy cream
- 1 teaspoon curry powder, Madras preferred
- 1 cup edible flowers (pansies, calendula, nasturtium)
- 1 dry hot chili (Thai, del arbor, habanero)
- 1 cup blended oil (soy-olive preferred)

SOUP: Peel the butternut squash and cut it in half. Use a soup spoon to scrape out all the seeds and cut each half in four even pieces. Peel the Spanish onion, cut in half and thinly slice.

Place a medium size pot over medium low heat, add 3 tablespoons of extra virgin olive oil and wait until hot. Add onions and sweat until nice and soft. Then add brown sugar, cinnamon, nutmeg, all spice and black pepper. Let the spices toast and stir with a wooden spoon until a beautiful aroma comes from the pot. Add the butternut squash and cover with hot water. Add salt. Place a lid on the pot and when it starts to boil, bring down to a very gentle simmer. Cook until you can pierce the butternut squash and there is no resistance. Strain and keep the cooking liquid. Add the butternut squash into a blender and add enough of the cooking liquid to blend. Be careful not to add too much liquid. Cool down in a double ice bath and refrigerate until ready to use.

MUSSELS: With a potato scrub, scrub the mussel shells and remove beard from each mussel. Place the mussels in a bowl, heat up a deep pot with a lid until it is smoking hot. Add ½ cup of water to the bowl with mussels and pour everything into the smoking hot pot. Cover with a lid until all the shells are open. As soon as they open, remove from the liquid to avoid overcooking. Remove the mussels from the shells and refrigerate until ready to use.

CRAB: Clean the meat and make sure there are no shells. Refrigerate the meat until ready to use.

TOASTED PUMPKIN SEEDS: Toast pumpkin seeds over medium heat in a sauté pan with one tablespoon of blended oil. Stir the seeds continuously in the pan to avoid burning and ensure that they are evenly toasted.

MANGO: Peel and dice the mango into cubes. Refrigerate until ready to use.

HYDRATED GOLDEN RAISINS: Place raisins into a container and cover with water. Wait for 12 hours before use. Raisins will be nice and plump. Drain and refrigerate until use.

CURRY CREAM: Mix 2 teaspoons of curry powder into 1/4 cup of water and stir until the curry powder dissolves.

Mix heavy cream and Crème Fraiche with the infused water. Stir until nice and smooth.

EDIBLE FLOWERS: This is an addition to the dish that gives beautiful variety of colors and fresh fragrant flavors. Pick the petals from the flowers very carefully and place on a damp paper towel until ready to use.

CHILI OIL: In a sauce pan over low heat, add one cup of blended oil and the hot chili. Let the chili infuse for ½ hour, then place oil and chili in a food processor and pulse until the chili is minced. Place in a container and reserve until ready to use. This chili oil can be stored for up to a month. Make sure to wash your hands well after handling the chili.

HERBS: Pick the leaves from the parsley and cilantro and place into a container with a damp paper towel on top until ready to use. Cut the chives into 1 inch sticks and keep them in a container with a damp towel on top until ready to use.

ASSEMBLY: Place the butternut puree into a medium sauce pan and bring to a simmer. Add mussels and turn the stove off. Let the soup sit for 1 minute to heat up the mussels. Ladle the soup into individual bowls. Each soup bowl should receive about five lumps of crab meat. Drizzle the curry cream on the soup surface. Then sprinkle the pumpkin seeds, dices of mango, golden raisins into the soup. Garnish each bowl with two leaves of each herb, 3 sticks of chives and edible flower petals. Finish with four to five drops of the spicy chili oil. The soup is your canvas for the other ingredients, have fun and bon appetite.

Seablue

Seablue, a Michael Mina restaurant, captivates diners with its eye-popping décor inspired by the Mediterranean Sea, exquisite service, interactive menu and exceptional cuisine. Whether you ask Executive Chef Biraj Patel to create the meal of your life by ordering his sampling menu or choose from the eclectic menu, it will be memorable.

Pristine seafood takes center stage here. Crab cakes are made with sweet Dungeness crab meat and served with a balsamic-marinated tomato and basil aioli. Delicious lobster corn dogs – mousseline of lobster wrapped around a stick, light-batter dipped and deep fried — show the chef's playful talents. A Mina classic – signature two-pound Maine lobster pot pie, with fingerling potatoes, haricot vert, baby carrots, English peas, and a truffled lobster cream sauce. Meat lovers will die for the Colorado rack of lamb off the wood-burning grill. Finish your exquisite meal with a touch of fun — a root beer float with warm chocolate chip cookies.

Come on in!

Address:

Borgata Hotel Casino & Spa
1 Borgata Way
Atlantic City

Phone:
866—MY BORGATA

Atlantic Monkfish Tagine

Ingredients / Serves 1

MONKFISH TAGINE
2 tablespoons canola oil
8 ounces marinated monkfish (2 ounce portion)
1 tablespoon garlic, chopped
3 ounces fish stock
2 ounces chermoula (recipe follows)
1 ounce marinated olives (Mix of kalamata and green)
1 ounce pickled tomatillas
1 ounce teardrop tomato
1 ounce roasted heirloom fingerling potato
1 ounce roasted eggplant
1 lemon wedge
Salt and white pepper to taste
2 sprigs parsley and chervil

CHERMOULA
8 each garlic cloves
½ cup parsley sprigs
⅓ cup cilantro sprigs
2 each lemon (zest of)
4 teaspoons paprika
2 teaspoons chili powder
2 teaspoons ground cumin
1 cup olive oil
Salt and pepper to taste

MONKFISH TAGINE: Marinade monkfish in chermoula sauce for 2 hours.

In a sauté pan, heat oil and add monkfish when oil is very hot and cook for 1 minute.

Add garlic and cook until it becomes fragrant.

Add fish stock and chermoula and mix well. Transfer to a tagine bowl or casserole dish.

Add the remaining ingredients and the juice of the lemon wedge and season with salt and pepper.

Cover and bake in a 350 degree oven for 5-6 minutes.

Garnish with herb sprigs.

Suggested Seafood alternative: Salmon, Prawns, or Black Bass.

CHERMOULA: Combine all ingredients in a blender and blend on low speed to puree. Add olive oil in a steady stream until it becomes a thick paste. Season with salt and pepper.

WINE: Qupé Syrah, Cuvée Michael Mina, Santa Barbara 2005.

Shanghai House

Shanghai House's dining room has a big Buddha in the center and a modern and ancient yin and yang cacophony that harkens back to Shanghai itself. Diners who choose to eat in are treated royally.

The all-inclusive menu has all the Chinese-American favorites, including truly great soups – egg-drop and hot-and-sour among them.

For a real treat, try the house duck, aptly dubbed a Chef's Specialty. No diner will be disappointed by this dish packed with jumbo shrimp, chicken pieces and roast pork pieces in a brown sauce with carrots, baby corn, Napa cabbage, broccoli florets and, of course, plenty of crisp breaded fried boneless duck.

Come on in!

Address:
28 East Maryland Avenue
Somers Point

Phone:
609-926-3388

Lovers Shrimp

Ingredients / Serves 1-2

16-20 tiger shrimp, cleaned
1 broccoli bunch
1 box spaghetti

GENERAL TSO'S SAUCE

3 teaspoons soy sauce
1 teaspoon oyster sauce
½ teaspoon ground bean sauce
3 teaspoons sugar
2 teaspoons vinegar
½ teaspoon garlic
½ teaspoon scallion
¼ teaspoon hot sauce
¼ cup chicken broth

SOMERS POINT SAUCE

½ cup mayonnaise
2 teaspoons orange juice
1 teaspoon Chinese liquid milk (found at any
    Asian supermarket)
Juice of ½ lemon

SHRIMP BATTER

¼ cup corn starch
egg white
¼ tsp salt
tsp oil
¼ cup water

GENERAL TSO'S SAUCE: Combine all ingredients and simmer on low until hot. To increase sauce thickness, add a little cornstarch.

SOMERS POINT SAUCE: Combine all ingredients and simmer until warm.

Cook spaghetti and set aside. Steam broccoli and set aside. Prepare both the General Tso's and the Somers Point sauces and set aside. Prepare shrimp batter. Dip cleaned shrimp into batter and place in wok fryer or fry in oil heated to 350 degrees until crispy and remove. Divide serving plate in half with pasta and steamed broccoli. Put equal amounts of shrimp on pasta and broccoli. Pour Somers Point sauce over one pile of shrimp and pour the General Tso's sauce over the remaining shrimp. You can garnish the plate with fresh orange wedges. Enjoy!

Steve & Cookie's By the Bay

Excellent food and music play a duet at Steve & Cookie's By the Bay. Local musical luminaries create a classic jazz nightclub atmosphere. Nightly music enhances the overall enjoyment of honest and straightforward food and service. Steve and Cookie Till's warm and inviting dining room overlooking the inland waterway draws a crowd in all seasons.

Delectable dishes include baked Maine lobster macaroni and cheese appetizer, a classic comfort food.

Bouillabaisse – shrimp, scallops, clams, crab meat, and Chilean sea bass served in a broth of saffron, tomato, fresh fennel, and anise, topped with a grilled slice of Tuscan bread and a squiggle of garlic mayonnaise — is a signature dish and deserves that status.

Rich cappuccino and key lime mousse pie are great ways to end a wonderful, musical meal. The new Oyster Bar is the place to see and be seen.

Come on in!

Address:
9700 Amherst Avenue
Margate

Phone:
609-823-1163

Web:
www.steveandcookies.com

Lobster Macaroni and Cheese

Ingredients / Serves 6-8

CHEESE SAUCE

1 quart heavy cream

1 quart half-and-half

2 cups whole milk

1 ¾ pound gruyere cheese

1 ¾ pound farmhouse cheddar

3 tablespoons Coleman's mustard powder

2 teaspoons white pepper

4 tablespoons Tabasco sauce

1/8 cup Worcestershire sauce

1 pound basic recipe roux — equal weights flour and butter

2 pounds cooked lobster, knuckle and claw meat

1 pound cooked orecchiette pasta

2 bundles finely chopped chives

PANKO BREAD CRUMBS

3 tablespoons unsalted butter

1 heaping teaspoon fresh garlic, finely minced

3 cups panko bread crumbs

parmesan cheese

SAUCE: In large saucepan bring liquids to simmer. Vigorously whisk in mustard powder and white pepper. Immediately at boiling point, whisk in enough roux until the cream is mayonnaise consistency. Reduce heat to low. Whisk in cheese, Worcestershire and Tabasco. Simmer for 15 minutes on very low heat, stirring frequently; avoid scorching. Salt to taste.

CRUMBS: In large sauté pan, melt butter and finely minced garlic. Add panko crumbs. Sauté until golden brown. Set aside and allow to cool.

ASSEMBLY: In a large mixing bowl, combine pasta, lobster meat, chives to taste and enough sauce to allow a saucy mixture. Transfer mix to casseroles. Top with a sprinkle of parmesan cheese and a full coating of crumbs. Bake at 400 degrees for three to four minutes until crumbs are golden.

The Gables

The Gables is romantic and sensuous, offering breakfast, lunch, afternoon tea, dinner, and after-theater supper. Chef Paul R. Simon also is an artist and turns each plate into his canvas.

Menus change daily, with the chef turning produce from local New Jersey farms, micro greens, organic meat and poultry, fresh diver scallops from Long Beach Island's surrounding waters, Prince Edward Island mussels, and lobsters from Maine into delectable dishes.

A selection of wines from New Jersey's Valenzano winery enhance the pleasure.

The Gables is housed in a meticulously refurbished Victorian structure. The dining room has pretty wooden floors and red walls. Tables also are set on the shady porch and in the enchanting Victorian garden courtyard, which features a sparkling fountain and a wealth of flowers.

Come on in!

Address:
212 Centre Street
Beach Haven

Phone:
888-LBI-GABLES

Web:
www.gableslbi.com

Shrimp with 3 Sauces

Herb Grilled Tiger Shrimp with Three Sauces and Crispy Prosciutto

Ingredients / Serves 4

1 pound (13-15) tiger shrimp, cleaned
4 thin slices prosciutto

BANANA SAUCE

1 banana
Juice of half a lime
1 clove garlic
½ cup mayonnaise
Salt and pepper

BASIL SAUCE

1 bunch basil
1 clove garlic
½ cup mayonnaise
Juice of half a lemon
Salt and pepper

SAFFRON PEPPER SAUCE

¼ cup quality roasted red peppers (piquillo preferred)
Pinch saffron
1 teaspoon sriracha pepper sauce
1 teaspoon sherry vinegar
½ cup mayonnaise

CRISPY PROSCIUTTO: Lay on Silpat or nonstick baking tray with another Silpat on top and bake at 350 degrees for 5-6 minutes until crispy.

SAUCES: Combine each one separately in a blender and puree until smooth. Reserve.

Season the shrimp with salt, pepper, and oil and grill or sauté.

PRESENTATION: Make three shrimp sized dots of sauce on each plate placing a shrimp on each sauce. Top each shrimp with a piece of crispy prosciutto.

WINE: Trimbach, Gewurztraminer

COOKING TIP: Use all your senses. Hear if it is cooking properly. You can usually smell something on the edge of burning oftentimes averting disaster.

The Inlet

A lovely view of the bay is a feast for the eyes at The Inlet. Sit on the deck for lunch or dinner and prepare to be wowed.

The menu is a coastal navigation chart of the area, offering plenty of appetizer choices, samplers, sandwiches, and entrée salads.

Both sea and land are represented. Some interesting choices include appetizers of tuna sliders, or seared spicy tuna burgers, and BBQ chicken spring rolls.

For entrees, tamarind-glazed Jail Island salmon and harissa-rubbed chicken are two standouts.

A wall of seashells, white beams with track lighting and muted colors add to The Inlet's comfortable elegance.

Come on in!

Address:
998 Bay Avenue
Somers Point

Phone:
609-926-9611

Crispy Jail Island Salmon

Coconut Lime Rice Roasted Pineapple Relish Wok Charred Vegetables

Ingredients / Serves 4

) 7 ounce Salmon fillets

each golden pineapple

hai basil, if available, if not field basil is good,
  chopped roughly

ounces Sweet rice wine (mirin)

red bell pepper, diced small

ounces rice vinegar

cup jasmine rice

ounces coconut milk

2 cup macadamia nuts, chopped and toasted

est of 1 lime

small onion, minced

tablespoons ginger, minced

tablespoon butter

cups chicken or vegetable broth

tablespoons olive oil

4 cup scallions, minced

tir fry vegetables

ounce sesame oil

ounce teriyaki sauce

each garlic clove, minced

alt (to season)

epper (to season)

RELISH: Peel and cut pineapple into ½ slices, salt and pepper each side and rub with a little bit of sesame oil and roast in the oven for 10-12 minutes, remove and let cool slightly and then dice each slice and place in a mixing bowl. Then to this add the sweet wine, vinegar, basil, and red pepper, check seasoning and set aside.

RICE: Sauté the onion and ginger in a small amount of butter and blended oil until translucent, about 4-5 minutes. Add the rice and stir to coat the rice with the oil and butter and then add the broth, coconut milk and season with salt and pepper. Cover the rice with foil and cook on low heat for 15 minutes or bake in the oven at 350 degrees covered for 20 minutes. After the alloted time let the rice sit covered for 5 minutes then remove cover and fluff with a fork and fold in macadamia nuts and scallions, set aside.

SALMON: Gently score the skin of the salmon with a sharp knife, but be careful not to cut too deep into the flesh. Season both sides with salt and pepper. Prepare a large sauté pan with olive oil and place on medium heat for 3-4 minutes. The oil should be hot enough at this point, you can test by placing a corner of the salmon in the pan if you hear "music" the pan is ready. Place the seasoned salmon skin side down in the pan and sear for 5-6 minutes, carefully turn the salmon over and place in a 375 degree oven for 4-5 minutes, the salmon should be medium rare to medium, this will depend on the thickness of the fish as well, if you like a more well done salmon just increase cooking time.

VEGETABLES: If available, prepare a wok with sesame oil (if not available, a large sauté pan will do) let it get hot for 2-3 minutes. Add the garlic and sauté for 15-20 seconds. Add the vegetables and cook for 1-2 minutes, so they are not overcooked. Add the teriyaki sauce and season with salt and pepper.

TO FINISH: Place the coconut rice down on the plate first then top with the wok charred vegetables, then top with salmon and spoon the relish over the salmon.

The Lobster House

The Lobster House has its own fleet of boats that haul fresh treasures of the sea to the restaurant and fish market. The freshness is just one reason the Lobster House is an institution.

Start with oyster stew, oysters lightly cooked until their delicate edges slightly curl, resting in a very creamy broth. Snapper soup is a dark version of very rich, thickened broth with tender shreds of meat and vegetables cooked until they melt in your mouth.

The Schooner Dinner is a metal kettle of steamers, mussels, shrimp, scallops and a one-pound split lobster steamed together in a mild broth and served with drawn butter for dipping. Simple and so good. Seafood served au natural is best. The Lobster House specialty is lobster tails, scallops and shrimp served over linguine with garlic butter sauce.

Come on in!

Address:
Fisherman's Wharf
Cape May Harbor

Phone:
609-884-8296

Web:
www.thelobsterhouse.com

Lobster House Specialty

(8) 2 ounce South African lobster tails
1 pound (31-35) shrimp
1 pound scallops
2 pounds linguine
8 garlic cloves, finely chopped
8 tablespoons butter
2 cups white wine
3 ounces oil
8 lemon wedges

Clean shrimp and scallops. Cut lobster tails with scissors down top part of shell. Open and pull tail meat out of shell almost all the way, then close shell and lay meat on top.

Heat oil until hot but not smoking. Place lobster tails in pan meat-side down. Add shrimp and scallops. Sauté on medium heat until golden brown. Add garlic, sweat for 30 seconds. Take pan off burner. Add wine, butter and juice from lemon wedges. Place on burner on high heat and let reduce until it thickens – about 6 or 7 minutes. Serve over linguine.

Tuckahoe Inn

Generations have enjoyed the views, ambience, and cuisine of the Tuckahoe Inn, overlooking the Great Egg Harbor Bay. Lunch, dinner, and cocktails all are served in a classy-but-unassuming setting.

French onion soup gratinee and crab artichoke dip are rich ways to start a meal. Sweet basil scallops, eight plump, juicy scallops over angel hair pasta, and filet mignon, broiled and served with sautéed mushrooms and a bearnaise sauce, are exquisite — full of flavor and fresh as could be.

Tuckahoe Inn is a great destination equally apropos for a date, celebrating an anniversary, or enjoying a special time with the whole family. Summertime, arrive by car or boat to enjoy the Back Bay Café, with a fun vibe and live music.

Come on in!

Address:
1 Harbor Road and Route 9
Beesleys Point

Phone:
609-390-3322

Web:
www.tuckahoeinn.com

Red Snapper Ponchatrain

Ingredients / Serves 4

pieces of red snapper fillet (we skin them by laying them flat on the cutting board skin side down starting at the tail run a sharp knife flat between the skin and the meat hold on to the skin so it doesn't slide.)

cup flour

eggs lightly beaten

tablespoon chopped parsley

ounces grated Romano cheese

nch of black pepper

ounces clarified butter or cooking oil

teaspoons of chopped shallots (red onion can be substituted)

cup of dry white wine (Chablis or whatever the cook likes to drink)

cup of chicken stock

uice of 1 lemon

ounces butter

ounces jumbo or lump crabmeat

ounces sliced almonds toasted

Combine eggs, cheese, parsley, and pepper to make a batter.

Heat oil in sauté pan large enough to fit the snapper fillets.

Lightly dredge snapper fillets in flour then in batter and place in pan. When edges start turning brown flip over and finish cooking. Remove and keep warm.

Add chopped shallots to pan, cook until translucent, deglaze with wine, add chicken stock and lemon juice.

Roll 1/2 of the butter in leftover flour and add to pan, cook until sauce starts to thicken. Add the crabmeat and the rest of the butter and heat through.

Plate the snapper, spoon sauce and crab meat over top, and garnish with toasted almonds.

WINE: Sonoma Valley Chardonnay

COOKING TIP: Between the time you say you'll cook something and the time you have to do it, you have time to learn how.

Conversion Table

1 cup	8 fluid ounces	1/2 pint	237 ml
2 cups	16 fluid ounces	1 pint	474 ml
4 cups	32 fluid ounces	1 quart	946 ml
2 pints	32 fluid ounces	1 quart	0.9 liters
4 quarts	128 fluid ounces	1 gallon	3.7 liters
8 quarts	256 fluid ounces	2 gallons	7.5 liters

Liquid Measurements

1 dash	6 drops
24 drops	¼ teaspoon
3 teaspoon	1 tablespoon
1 tablespoon	½ fluid ounce
2 tablespoon	1 fluid ounce
½ cup	4 fluid ounces
16 tablespoon	1 cup
1 cup	½ pint
2 cups	1 pint
2 pints	1 quart
4 quarts	1 gallon

Common Abbreviations

tsp	teaspoon
tbs.	tablespoon
c	cup
oz	ounce
pt	pint
lb	pound
qt	quart